GIGANTIC:
The Story of
FRANK BLACK & THE
PIXIES

John Mendelssohn

OMNIBUS PRESS

LONDON / NEW YORK / PARIS / SYDNEY / COPENHAGEN / BERLIN / MADRID / TOKYO

Exclusive Distributors:
Music Sales Limited,
14/15 Berners Street,
London W1T 3LJ.

Music Sales Corporation,
257 Park Avenue South,
New York, NY 10010, USA.

Macmillan Distribution Services,
53 Park West Drive,
Derrimut, Vic 3030,
Australia.

Every effort has been made to trace the copyright holders of the photographs in this book
but one or two were unreachable. We would be grateful if the photographers concerned
would contact us.

Typeset by Galleon Typesetting, Ipswich.
Printed by Mackays of Chatham plc, Chatham, Kent.

A catalogue record for this book is available from the British Library.

Visit Omnibus Press on the web at www.omnibuspress.com

For Claire and Brigitte

Boundless love also to my friends Big Screen Rumsey,
nancy hoagland rumsey, Toni Emerson, Peter Pacey,
Mark Pringle, Kathleen Guneratne,
Stiofan Lanigan-O'Keeffe, Anna Chen, and Lil P,
and to my sister Lori.

Contents

"From the word go, from the very first gig we played, people clapped. We played a couple of gigs and were on our way to Amsterdam. We were very fortunate."

– Charles Thompson

1

Hating That Bitch

A PORT city on the southern California coast about a third of the
way between Los Angeles (known for its tawdry glamour) and
San Diego (known for its perfect climate), Long Beach has for much
of its history been known as a Navy town. As such, it has traditionally had a disproportionate number of adult bookstores, tattoo
parlours (this well before the Stray Cats' Brian Setzer single-handedly
made tattoos safe for rock'n'roll) and military surplus stores. No
rocker of note has ever grown up there, but the horrid harbour city
of San Pedro, around seven miles west and a little bit south, would in
the late Seventies cough up The Minutemen, whose songs made
those of The Ramones seem like Yes in comparison. Hawthorne,
around 15 minutes north if there was no traffic, had in the previous
decade given us The Beach Boys. It was in Long Beach that Charles
Michael Kittridge Thompson IV, on the spelling of whose second
middle name no two people agree, was born early in the spring of
1965, the year that Bob Dylan and The Byrds were widely accused
of having invented folk rock.

While still an infant, he would later tell interviewers – though it's
difficult to imagine him actually remembering the incident – his
parents took him via a suspiciously circuitous route to San Francisco,
stopping one afternoon at some cousins' house in the small north
central Nebraska town of Alliance. A large, reddish-orange, saucer-
shaped ship with portholes suddenly appeared in the late-afternoon
pre-dusk sky, and floated there for some 15 minutes. Alarmed, the
family notified the police, who came out for a look themselves, and

then tried unsuccessfully to follow the spaceship when it got bored and buggered off.

Not all of Charles' childhood memories would be so happy. Indeed, one of the first Christmas Eves he can remember, his grandmother pointed up at a red light in the sky (probably a little aeroplane's brake lights) and told him it was Rudolph the Red-Nosed Reindeer, guiding Santa's sleigh down to Charles. He scurried in terror to his bed and hid trembling under the covers, only for Grandma, unaware of his terror, to tiptoe out onto the balcony outside his window and shake sleighbells.

For a long while thereafter, the mere mention of the jolly fat gift-giver was enough to paralyse him with dread. He spent the subsequent Christmas Eve lying awake in bed in his own cold sweat, dreading the awful sound of hooves on the roof. Understandably, there are no known photographs of him as a small child sitting contentedly on the lap of some disgruntled underemployed borderline alcoholic actor paid peanuts to impersonate jolly St. Nick at Del Amo Fashion Center, and not only because America's second largest mall didn't actually open, just a very few miles from Charles' birthplace, until 1975.

His early boyhood memories also include glimpsing things in the sky that he felt sure weren't ordinary aeroplanes, and might very well have been . . . UFOs! On one memorable occasion, he and his younger brother Errol both observed what he would later describe as "a rocket-shaped craft" passing silently overhead while they were outside playing. Both boys stopped to watch, and then, being little fellows, got back to the important business of playing. Neither talked about the incident to anyone, not even to each other, until it came up quite by chance some 25 years later in conversation. Each thought it was his own weird personal memory, and was flabbergasted to discover that his brother remembered the same event. When extraterrestrials came to be Charles' fallback topic, that which he wrote about when he had to come up with lyrics quickly, he would concede that his family's having lived near the Goodyear blimp's launch site in Carson might have had much to do with his multiple sightings.

In any event, he wasn't yet out of kindergarten when he first heard rock'n'roll's siren song. "There was a guy who played drums down the street in his basement," he recalled. "I didn't even know what a drum set was – I didn't even know what it was when I looked at it! I just heard it and it was like, 'What's that? I want to be around that!'".

Little Charles never had a chance to get too comfortable or otherwise in the city of his birth. Four times before he graduated from high school, he moved back and forth between America's coasts with his younger brother Errol, mother and stepfather, attending 10 different schools ranging, according to how much real estate his realtor stepdad was managing to sell at the time, from private schools to gritty inner city ones. It was enough to make a little fellow's head spin. He found some small solace in the New York naïf Melanie's 'Brand New Key', which some believe, albeit without documentation, to be a greater crime against humanity than even Peter, Paul & Mary's 'Puff The Magic Dragon'.

Moving back to California without extensive premeditation around the time of his eighth birthday, Charles' parents gave away his entire Beatles collection. He was appropriately devastated, but sufficiently recovered within a year to make his first known musical performance – of Woody Guthrie's 'Why Oh Why' – in a Unitarian church in Boston, as half of a duet with a chum whose affluent hippie parents belonged to the quaintly named Boston Folk Song Society.

Having been encouraged by his mum to play records rather than sit staring moronically at television like most American children, he'd earlier (as a 4th grader) discovered Bob Dylan, and thought, "What's *this* all about?" He'd enjoyed detecting a subtle, appealing note of foreboding – "a good sadness, a beautiful sadness," he would sigh reminiscently decades later – in Peter, Paul & Mary's version of '500 Miles'.

At one point, his family moved into a flat whose previous occupant had left behind a copy of The Beatles' 'Let It Be', which Charles, preferring the zany, anarchic 'You Know My Name', is thought to have mistaken as the record's B-side. It is unknown if Charles is one of those who believes it would be a far, far better world if, at the end of every benefit concert ever held in Britain, the massed celebrities on stage sang 'You Know My Name' rather than Paul McCartney's much better-known vague ode to hopefulness.

Later songs of his own composition such as the Pixies' 'There Goes My Gun' would suggest that, when he investigated The Beatles further, he was much taken with the insistent simplicity of the lyrics of such of their songs as 'Why Don't We Do It In The Road?'

When Charles was 12, his parents joined the Pentecostal church, a charismatic denomination known in appreciable part for its appeal to the slightly unbalanced, such as those who are certain that Procter & Gamble is secretly controlled by Satan. There's much shouting about fire and brimstone at Pentecostal services, and not a little talking in tongues (though anyone with any sense at all would agree that English is God's language). Charles was forever being uprooted, he was about to experience the ravages of puberty, and here those whom he trusted most had thrown in with some of the wackiest zealots in the religious firmament. It was enough to make a boy's head spin.

He was sent for 7th and 8th grades to a Christian school in Downey, home turf of Karen and Richard Carpenter. His new school had so few able-bodied boys that its baseball coach, desperate to field a complete team, bribed the reluctant Charles to be part of it. If Charles would play ball, so to speak, the coach would allow him to borrow from his collection of 5,000 record albums. Thus did Charles come to develop a taste for such white blues giants as Paul Butterfield and John Mayall. He began checking blues albums out of the library. He saw a performance by the flaxen-haired Christian rock god Larry Norman and was impressed by a song that exhorted the listener to "come on, pilgrim!"

It is the Lord's will that teenaged males yearn fervently to squirt their seed into teenaged and other females. By his own reckoning, Charles wanted to do so even more than most, but it had been the Lord's will to make him enormously unprepossessing physically – Charles Schulz's Charlie Brown made flesh. He found some small solace in the recordings of Leon Russell, and in Lillian Roxon's *Rock Encyclopedia*, not caring that, for instance, it celebrated the exemplarily tasteful drumming on Bob Dylan tracks which contained no drumming. He did some drumming of his own, on a little drum kit he'd managed to put together – not to Butterfield's 'Born In Chicago', oddly, but Donovan's 'Mellow Yellow'. Then a cousin who sometimes stayed with his family left his classical guitar behind, but not before showing Charles how to play G, B, and A chords (if only she'd thrown in either a D or E, he could have played a 12-bar blues!). Charles began to dream of one day being in a band. If only his mum and stepfather would stay put!

One epochal afternoon – the exact date unknown, all these decades later, even to the principals – a former Thai pop musician neighbour noticed Charles with guitar and a Beatles songbook in hand, and invited him over to make a little home recording of Paul McCartney's coy imitation of John Lennon at his earthiest and most primal, 'Oh! Darlin'', from *Abbey Road*. "Come on, Chuck!" he implored when Charles sang it rather more as Donovan might have. "Sing it like you hate that bitch!"

This moment ranks in rock history near The Kinks' Dave Davies discovering that his naff little amplifier sounded a lot more interesting if he punctured its speaker's cone with knitting needles, with Mick Jagger's discovering that, if he pretended to be a 55-year-old black Southern sharecropper rather than a spotty 20-year-old London School of Economics student when he sang, no one died laughing, with Eddie Van Halen's discovering hammering on, with Grand Wizzard Theodore inventing what the hip hop community came to know as scratching.

It's interesting to note that it might never have taken place – and thus one of rock'n'roll's most memorable signature sounds not been fomented – had not the former Thai pop musician made a fundamental mistake. The singer in 'Oh! Darlin'' doesn't hate the lover to whom he's singing. Far, far from it! He pleads with her not to abandon him, suggesting that if she does so, it will kill him.

For this misapprehension, Lord, we thank Ye.

Or maybe the afternoon was more apocryphal than epochal, in which case the accounts we should believe are those in which the Thai musician works by day with Charles in a flower shop and exhorts him, as a matter of policy, not to sing just Paul McCartney's song 'Oh! Darlin'' as though he hated that bitch, but to sing everything requiring a little extra oomph as Paul McCartney had sung 'Oh! Darlin''.

Be that as it may, time passed. Charles' mum bought him a ticket to a Jethro Tull concert for his 14th birthday. There are those who might describe this as child abuse, but we must assume that she was trying, in her way, to be generous. Listening to 'Aqualung', Charles realised that tempos are there to be tampered with.

He discovered Hüsker Dü, a punk-inspired trio from Minneapolis that, along with The Minutemen, R.E.M., Black Flag, The Meat Puppets, and The Replacements, was coming to dominate the nation's college radio airwaves, and demonstrating that a band didn't have to be Foreigner or Boston to make a living. He gravitated naturally to the misfits at whatever school he happened to have been consigned to, persons who listened to music antithetical to that popular at the mall, as Charles might have too if his budget hadn't restricted him almost exclusively to used records. Not for Charles the latest Ramones album, or Devo. For poor Charles, who made a few extra bucks working on an archaeological dig in Arizona, Ten Years After and the dreadful first Cat Stevens album, recorded before he even had a beard. It is widely believed that he attended Narbonne High School in the South Bay, near Long Beach, a school whose chief distinction is that its name rhymes with Darvon, a popular, though highly addictive, narcotic analgesic.

2

(Vicky's Story)
The Saddest Thing I'd Ever Heard

MY dad has all these photos of himself on the walls of his apartment that you'd never in a million years guess are him. A year before I was born, he was in this band in Boston, The Lids, and they all looked exactly like Johnny Ramone, with their fringes touching their upper eyelids, except in like psychedelic clothes – paisley and polka dot shirts, plaid trousers, and these weird little sunglasses with lenses the size of a postage stamp.

They're snarling in the photos, according to my dad, as like a reaction to the tradition of singers always feeling they needed to look in their official portraits like they just won the lottery or something. In the photos of the early Beatles he's shown me, they're either grinning these big cheesy grins (not such a good idea in George's case, not with those North of England working class teeth!) or literally jumping up in the air they're so chuffed about something. But The Rolling Stones always looked like they wanted to cut the photographer's heart out, and The Lids were very majorly into the Stones. Whenever a new Stones album came out, in fact, they'd all drive down to New York together to buy the latest Stones-type fashions at this place in the Lower East Side – even, I guess, if the Stones were wearing plaid trousers.

At one time, to advertise itself or something, one of the big radio stations here in Boston used to leave stacks of their new Boss 30 on the counters of like record stores every Friday afternoon for punters to take home. My dad's got the one from November 5, 1966, with The Lids' 'Stop Cheating On Me' at number 19. But then the next week two of them were like arrested for possession of dangerous drugs (cannabis was a big deal in Boston in those days, apparently), and the next week southern New England stopped hearing 'Stop Cheating On Me' on the radio. The lead singer had to cut his hair short for his court appearance, and the group had to wait like three months before they could play in public again, and by that time there was this thing called the Bosstown Sound happening, and The Lids were suddenly like old-fashioned.

My dad's pretty bitter about that. He says that none of the groups that were supposed to be the best of the Bosstown Sound had actually been seen in any of the clubs The Lids played at, and that they were mostly like lame imitations of San Francisco hippie bands.

He went to London to see if he could get in like a proper English group, but got drafted. He managed to get my mum pregnant with me just before he flew back to Boston to be inducted into the army and sent to Viet Nam. He wasn't one of those guys who came home mad – the army had a band, and if he wasn't quite good enough to play in it, he was certainly good enough to set up the drums and amplifiers and everything.

It wasn't Viet Nam that drove him mad, but my mom's dying when I was nine. My dad got like majorly depressed after that, and I had to be put in foster care for a while until he finally snapped out of it. When we moved back to Boston and he married Nanci (I tried with all my might to talk her out of the idea at the end, but it was no use), both of us were happy. I'd always felt I was missing out not having a sibling to torture and like take things out on, and Nanci's daughter Tricia, two years younger than me, was just what the doctor ordered – the suffer-in-silence kind, the kind who never fights back. But when Nanci disappeared (not like kids on the sides of milk cartons, but after leaving a note that said, "I want my life back") around 18 months ago, my dad was back to having no wife and two daughters, one of them not even his, to worry about, and he started hitting the bottle pretty hard. He devoted his own life to sitting in front of the TV surrounded by a growing collection of empty beer cans.

He'd always taken a lot of pride in his appearance, but he like let himself go big time. What was left of his hair got greasy, and all he ever wore anymore were ratty old sweatpants and T-shirts that had stains from like every meal he'd ever eaten, and he didn't smell so good, believe me. I actually felt kind of guilty leaving him in that state when I moved into my own place (well, shared with a room-mate) in Cambridge. The first month or two, I was back to visit him like once a week, though, after realising that me and my roommate, on a scale of one to 100, with 100 being identical twins, had like minus–1,000 in common.

I happened to be over there the night of Tricia's first date – or what should have been Tricia's first date. I knew something was up the minute I walked in because the place smelled like an old hippie head shop or something. Tricia was burning enough incense to deodorise half of Eastie. It wouldn't do, I guess, for her date to come in and get a whiff of Dad, who she'd even got to put on real trousers – faded black jeans – and a real shirt, with a collar and buttons and sleeves. Most remarkable of all, he was drinking a Diet Pepsi. I couldn't remember when I'd seen him with a can of anything other than beer in hand.

Not that he was happy about it. Can you guess the first words out of his mouth when I came in? No, not his usual, "Yo, Vic," but, "But why can't I have just one? Whose friggin' house is it anyway?" And this directed not to me, but to the queen of the prom herself, who looked so clueless in the first makeup she'd probably ever tried to put on that I just wanted to throw my arms around her.

"Because, Paul, like we've already discussed," she told my dad in the tone of a mom talking to a four-year-old, "it just won't do for you to reek of beer when he shows up. You'll have all night after we leave to drink as much as you please."

"What's that supposed to mean?" my dad demanded. "That you think you're going to stay out until all hours? Well, you can forget about that right here and now, young lady."

Young lady! My dad trying to be like all paternal, laying down the law! Now it was him I wanted to throw my arms around.

"And wasn't he supposed to be here by now?"

Tricia looked at her wristwatch. What it said didn't please her. She tried to take a bite out of one of her fingernails – and this a girl who once like completely mortified me, saving up for like six weeks to have fake fingernails put on at one of those parlours with little Oriental women dying slow deaths breathing chemical fumes! It was 7.45.

"Let's see what's on the news," I said. "Maybe they've sussed why Challenger blew up. I'm willing to bet it was something really small and stupid, somebody forgetting to tighten a nut or something." Tricia didn't look even a little bit distracted. You could tell it was taking every bit of her will power to keep from checking her wristwatch again and seeing that it was now less than one minute later than the last time she looked.

"How about this?" my dad said, suddenly looking like really pleased with himself. "Where did Christa McAuliffe vacation this year? Tricia? Any guesses?"

She just glared at him, and then couldn't keep from looking at her wristwatch. "I don't know," she said, working on her fingernail again. "Where?"

"You know who I mean, right?" my dad, who's like almost 40, but who never quite got his head round the idea of making sure your audience knows who you're talking about *before* you tell the joke, thought to ask. "That schoolteacher who was killed when Challenger . . ."

"I know who she is, Paul," Tricia interrupted him, like snarling. "Jesus. Everybody in America knows who she is."

"All over Florida."

"Huh?"

"All over Florida," my dad said. "Is where Christa McAuliffe took her vacation this year. Do you get it?"

Tricia gave him a look like it was him she wanted to take a bite out of. She looked at her wristwatch again and gasped in pain. "Twenty-two minutes late now," she said. "He's probably not coming at all."

"You know how unreliable the T can be," my dad said. "He's probably on the train right now, worrying you're going to be pissed off at him for being late. Come have a seat, why don't you?"

Instead, she charged into her bathroom, slammed the door, and wailed. My dad and I looked at each other. He shrugged. "Christ," he said. "What I'd do for a beer. And what if the little shitrag doesn't show up at all? Can you imagine how hurt she's apt to be?"

My dad's memory seems to get shorter and shorter. It wasn't two years ago that I was the one like dying a thousand deaths waiting for the guy who was supposed to be taking me on my first date. And he never did. And me 17 years old at the time, a year older than Tricia. Oh, really cool, finally getting asked on your first date at 17, except not really because the guy decides at the last minute to stay home with like a jar of Vaseline and the latest issue of *Penthouse* or something.

I was too big. I *am* too big. Five-ten and a half, and that's if I don't stand up perfectly straight. And not naturally feminine, no shrinking violet. And it might have been majorly cool at one time to have an English accent in Boston, but all it did for me was make me seem even more a freak. My second week of high school, these two boys pretended to be gorillas on either side of me, like pounding their chests, as I walked down the hall. A lot of kids found it really hilarious. I found it like mortifying, but should have tried to pretend I was in on the joke or something, instead of bloodying the nose of the bigger one.

The boys at my school much preferred the little Pat Benatar types in spandex and legwarmers and big hair to a girl who bloodied the noses of boys who teased her and was going without lunch trying to save enough money to have her one huge long eyebrow electrolysised. And then it got round that, instead of just doing like the traditional feminine thing after getting stood up – slashing my own wrists, or overdosing on my mum's Valium, or, at the very least, crying myself to sleep – I hunted the little dickhead down, and I could pretty much count on not being asked out ever again.

I'd thought me and Cory had a lot in common. We were both like serious misfits, the misfits not even other misfits liked. What we were going to do on our date was listen to tapes of cool new indie bands at his uncle's place. His uncle was going to be out of town for the weekend. If it had been anybody else, I would have said no, expecting to be raped, but Cory seemed like asexual, and he couldn't have overpowered me if there'd been three of him, unless he spiked my drink or something, and I planned to make him take a big swig of anything he offered me.

To his small credit, he phoned 40 minutes after he was meant to have collected me to say he'd changed his mind, but that didn't really help much. And that was literally what he said – "I've changed my mind about like going out with you." He didn't have the decency to pretend something had come up, or that his uncle had stayed in town or something. And I did cry myself to sleep. But Nanci had buggered off by that time, and hadn't been the sort to take Valium in the first place, so instead of topping myself, I found Cory and his two mates at lunch the next day.

For a long time, he pretended he didn't see me, which would have been a pretty good trick, since I was standing right in front of him, deliberately casting a shadow across his little weasel face. Finally, one of his mates said, "Someone to see you, I think, Cory." Cory gave me this really hateful look, the kind most teenagers save for their parents when they like tell them they can't do a particular thing. I grabbed his sandwich out of his hand, opened it up (a single slice of this vile grey lunchmeat, with a knackered-looking tomato slice and some limp lettuce), and tried to stick the two halves to the sides of his head. His mates ran off in like terror. It was pretty funny, and actually gave me quite a lot of pleasure, though for the next month or so when I'd come down the hall the clever dicks would make a big show of getting out of my way, like infant school kids avoiding somebody with the lurgy.

Then, after I'd like resigned myself to never going out on a date, this guy with totally repulsive acne, Ryan, who somehow managed to be on the football team and put the shot for the track and field team without being popular with other jocks, told me before Biology one day that he thought what I'd done was awesome.

I'd never seen anybody blush like that. It wasn't just like every drop of blood in his own body had rushed to his face, which you could just barely make out for the oozing craters, but every drop of blood of everybody in the class. Which was probably why he wasn't popular with the other jocks.

Like most kids in high school who aren't going to be asked, or who don't have the cheek to ask, I pretended I didn't have any interest in the prom, but I did. I like majorly wanted to go. And then, around 48 hours beforehand, weeks after the little spandex cutie-pies had started planning what they were going to wear, and what to do with their hair, and which of their mums' jewellery to borrow, Ryan asked me, blushing so hard I thought his poor face might explode.

When he restored my faith in the male half of humanity by actually turning up on the night, in a rented white dinner jacket that wasn't quite big enough for him even though it was the biggest one they'd had, my dad tried to bum a cigarette, but Ryan didn't smoke. He even apologised for his own dad's dented Cadillac smelling of cigars.

The prom wasn't fun at all. I thought about all the tens of thousands of kids all over New England who were like boiling themselves in self-hatred because they hadn't gone, and how nobody should have suffered for like a millisecond about missing something so retarded. I was pretty sure the real jocks, the ones who could talk to girls without their faces turning bright colours, and their little cutie-pie girlfriends, were snickering at us. We tried dancing, but it was like a disaster. I yelped so loud when Ryan stepped on my feet (and at one point it was like he was trying to, I swear) that other couples gave us dirty looks, like we were ruining their enchanted evening or something.

We couldn't think of much to say to each other. He collected World War II stuff and didn't like music enough to have a favourite group. It didn't like occur to him that asking who mine was might really get the conversational ball rolling. He excused himself every ten minutes or so, to go to what he called "the little boys' room". His bladder must have been the same size as one of the little Pat Benatar clones'. People who say "little boys' room" and "little girls' room" have always made me want to like put my finger down my throat, just to speed things along, if you know what I mean.

At the end, they played 'Nights In White Satin', and all the little Pat Benatar clones got like all dewy-looking, like they planned to remember the moment for the rest of their lives. We'd already tried dancing, and it had been a disaster. So I was relieved when he didn't ask me to dance – and amazed when he asked instead if I might like to go up to this place he knew that had like a really romantic view of downtown Boston. I figured kissing him would be about as sexy as lowering my face into a bowl of pus, but I said OK anyway. I didn't want to seem like an ingrate.

He sucked so many mints on the way up that you couldn't smell his dad's cigar smoke anymore. I asked if we could have some music. I kept hearing 'Nights In White Satin' – the part where the dude sings, "I love you-oo" like really high and fervently – and it was driving me crazy. The radio was playing something really lame, but Ryan wasn't allowed to change the channel. "Dad made me promise," he said. Like it would be a major inconvenience to punch the button or something.

We got there. It was like trying to find a place downtown on Saturday afternoon – teeming. He found one, though, set the hand brake and turned toward me all flushed with lust or something. I asked if we couldn't just look at the view. He took it to mean that he hadn't had enough mints, and broke open a fresh roll. I wondered what it would be like to be on a date with someone you like really fancied, and hated the petite little sexpots in the cars to either side of us. Why them and not me? Had I asked to be big?

When I said, "Well, maybe I'd better get home now," I felt an idiot. Like I had big plans for the morning after my senior prom or something! And then he was all over me, trying to get his tongue in my mouth, grabbing at me with what seemed like four hands. I had to poke him hard between the legs to get him to stop.

He looked surprised and hurt, and then angry. He sat there seething for a minute, and then blurted. "Don't you think you owe me something? How would you have gone to the prom without me? I've just done you the biggest favour of your life, you ungrateful bitch."

A big part of me wanted to jump out of the car and find my own way home, but it was chilly, and I didn't think I'd get very far either in my majorly uncomfortable heels or barefoot. I told him I thought it was me who'd done the bigger favour, accepting his invitation.

"You're putting me on!" he like sputtered. "Do you honestly think anybody else would have asked you?" He grabbed his rearview mirror and tilted it for me. "Just take a fuckin' look at yourself, will you?"

I grabbed the mirror and tilted it toward him and told him to take his own advice. I called him Pizzaface, and immediately felt bad about it, like I was hitting him below the belt. We just sat there glaring at each other while on both sides of us more petite, less bolshy girls were letting boys with less gross complexions unhook their brassieres. We glared holes in each other, and then burst into laughter.

The cool punchline would be that each of us like realised that we really liked the other after all, and lost our virginity up there in his back seat, and went on to be girlfriend and boyfriend, not giving a toss if anybody snickered at how we looked together. But we didn't. After we stopped laughing, we realised each of us found the other pretty gross, and it wasn't like he had a sparkling engaging personality or anything, so he drove me home, not even bothering to get out of the car at the end, and I never saw him again.

It was now ten past eight, there was still no sign of Tricia's date, and the sound of Tricia sobbing in the loo had Dad saying, as he didn't when it was me it was happening to, "If he doesn't show up, Vic, I swear to Christ I'll go to her school and find out where he lives. If I hurt the kid, they can put me in jail, so it's his old man I'll hurt – bad." You could have said it was the beer talking, except he'd only just realised there was nothing keeping him from it anymore, gone to the fridge, and got himself one, which he'd only had a couple swigs of. I don't think my dad had ever been in a fight in his life, or at least one he'd won.

I tried to get in to comfort Tricia when she moved from the loo to what had become her bedroom, rather than ours, when I moved out. "Fuck off," she shrieked when I tapped on the door, "just fuck right off, will you?"

It was the first time I'd ever heard her use a four-letter word. It was the saddest thing I'd ever heard.

3

Hummus for Hellions

BY 1983, Charles was a freshman anthropology major at the University of Massachusetts, living in an on-campus dormitory (whose other inhabitants, including J. Macsis, later of Dinosaur Jr. fame, already notable for his Cure-derived coiffure, were not delighted by the unusual pungency of his feet), and getting the impression that he might have something major in common with another of his suitemates, a freshman economics major from Manila by way of Yonkers, New York – Joseph Alberto Santiago.

The Santiagos had once enjoyed extraordinary wealth and privilege – of the first three Mercedes imported into the Philippines, Joey's uncle had got two, twice as many as President Ferdinand Marcos. But then, in the wake of a number of terrorist bombings in Manila (many of which he was later discovered to have sponsored), Marcos was able to acquire dictatorial power, and Joey's anaesthetist father decided his family would be better off in America.

The third of six sons, Joey was said to have cycled a very great distance, if not across the continent, on behalf of charity – and then not been arsed to collect the money his heroism had raised. He admitted to having chosen to study at U-Mass in significant part because it was far enough from Yonkers for him to have to live on campus.

Just as Charles had once tapped along with 'Mellow Yellow', so Joey had taught himself to play lead guitar over the two chords of Donovan's 'Sunshine Superman'. Charles found him strangely gnomic. At times, it was almost as though he were speaking in riddles, and Charles wouldn't have any idea of what Joey had been saying until 10 minutes after their conversation ended. But all reservations fell by the wayside when they got out their guitars and began to play 'In The Midnight Hour', which Charles was later said to have sung at his high school's senior prom. (If so, remarkable – first because he attended it in the first place [kids whose parents moved around a lot traditionally stayed alone at home and masturbated bitterly on prom night], and second because Wilson Pickett's celebration of the joys of deferred lust wasn't exactly 'Nights In White Satin' as a prom favourite.)

From the first moment, right after they admitted to each other that they'd come to college mostly in hopes of starting bands, it somehow seemed just right that they should be playing together. Charles had already composed the riff to what would become entitled 'U-Mass' and that with which 'Levitate Me' would begin. Joey, for his part, had learned an odd but viable alternative to normal guitar tablature from one of those grizzled student lifers one meets at college, an Amish-looking fellow going for something on the order of his fifth doctorate. "We got talking," Joey would later marvel, "and it turned out that he played guitar too. He showed me this way of writing down shapes and notes that wasn't like normal tablature."

There are those Pixies apologists who believe that Joey was already well into all the hippest bands, and others who believe that he was hardly more conversant with those bands in the early days of their friendship than Charles himself was. What everyone agrees is that it wasn't long before the two new friends were listening to Iggy's *Lust For Life*, Hüsker Dü, Violent Femmes, The Replacements, and, from the previous decade, the strange band from Rhode Island that had inspired so many of them, Talking Heads. Charles liked Violent Femmes for their nerdy angst and sexual frustration, and was even more taken with the ambiguity of Iggy's sneering persona – never knowing for sure whether Iggy was mocking himself, the listener, the song, or all three struck the blond freshman as strangely enjoyable.

('Tis a funny thing, rock'n'roll, and make no mistake. At the time of their emergence, slightly before Charles began kindergarten, Iggy's band The Stooges, over whose numbskull hard rock riffing Iggy did the world's most brazen Mick Jagger imitation, had struck nearly everyone as a joke. Those who didn't get it stuck with The Moody Blues or Crosby, Stills & Nash or something, while those who did immediately formed bands of their own [it took around 25 minutes to become as accomplished a guitarist as Scott Asheton, fewer if you didn't wear an outfielder's mitt on your left hand]. The author, he pauses to note, was one of those who got it, and in a big way, after seeing Iggy gnawing the shoes of members of the audience at the Whisky-a-Go-Go in Los Angeles, and thinking, "Rock'n'roll!")

But the pleasure Charles derived from getting baked (on cannabis) and either listening to records with Joey or playing guitar with him wasn't enough to keep him in Amherst when he was offered an opportunity, as part of a student exchange programme, to study for a year either in Puerto Rico or at Cork University in Ireland. Whether it was the lure of Caribbean sunshine or the prospect of getting really good at Spanish (as what freshman anthro major doesn't yearn to be?) that made him choose the former has been tepidly debated by Thompson biographers for years. What is known for sure is that he was soon in the Rio Piedras district of San Juan, and ravenous, as his Spanish wasn't yet good enough to open a bank account and cash a cheque. When he was finally able to do so, he bought himself a heaping portion of rice and black beans, a dish for which he would come to harbour such adoration that he later named his music publishing company in its honour.

Black beans and rice, though, turned out to be just about the only thing Puerto Rican he really liked. "There are probably far worse places in the world," he would later concede to an Irish interviewer, "but Puerto Rico is weird . . . because it's American! It's a welfare state, so the people are really screwed up – they've been on the dole for something like 500 years . . . And they've got a really bad identity problem. Some of them want to be Indian, but more think of themselves as American. And because it's essentially Catholic, that fucks things up even more. The serious alcohol problems don't help much either."

On discovering that a great, great many of his fellow residents in the high-rise *hospedaje* in which he'd been bivouacked were gay – and not the nice, quiet, maybe even slightly stand-offish kind who spend their time working out to the accompaniment of Donna

Summer records or developing exquisite taste, but instead real
screamers given to dressing like Carmen Miranda and wearing lurid
fingernail polish – Charles took to trying to work up an alcohol
problem of his own, seeking refuge from his apparently psychotic
roommate (the inspiration of the Pixies song 'Crackity Jones') and
the dormitory's general Roman bathhouse ambience not only on the
beach, but in bars. There was only so much time one could spend on
a beach with so few tapes to listen to – a Ramones album, and
Talking Head's *Little Creatures*, but none of the Iggy stuff he'd
thought he'd taped. He toyed with the idea of flying to New
Zealand on his dad's tab for the once-in-a-lifetime thrill of observing
the passing of Halley's comet from the best vantage point on earth. It
seemed a cool, romantic thing to do.

Most fathers, on getting wind of their first-born sons' decisions to
drop out of college (and thus throw their whole lives away), would
react by threatening to disown the ungrateful little rotters, rather
than fly them around the world. We must therefore assume that a
thick string was attached to Charles' offer – perhaps Charles would
have to promise, on getting back from Down Under, to get five doc-
torates? What we know for fact is that he decided in the end against
astronomy, and for rock'n'roll, and sent Mr. Joseph A. Santiago,
temporarily of Amherst, Massachusetts, a letter imploring him to
take a similar leap of faith.

Depending on whose reminiscences you trust, Mr. Joseph A.
Santiago either immediately endorsed the idea, or needed to be
coaxed and cajoled for a couple of weeks, but in either event he and
Charles soon found themselves sleeping side by side in a van parked
behind a Boston Dunkin' Donuts. They got jobs in waterfront ware-
houses – Joey's full of butcher block furniture, Charles' of buttons –
and rented the squalid digs that tradition prescribes for the not-yet-
famous.

Watching local bands, they determined that 40 minutes was about
the optimum length for a set. They agreed that watching some other
guitarist's fingers flying nimbly up and down his or her fretboard was
boring, and that their band would play no solos. Liking the way that
resolution made them feel, they resolved next to cut out nothing less
than anything heard before – an extremely tall order in view of the

fact that it's nearly impossible to play rock'n'roll without including the occasional A-major chord, for instance, or four big beats to the bar. But this was no time for quibbling!

"When you first start out," Charles would explain years later, "you're afraid to sound traditional or formulaic 'cause you're afraid of just sounding really bland. So you do something more esoteric. It wasn't about how we wanted to sound and our 'musical vision'. It was about what we didn't want to sound like – whatever they were playing on MTV or on the radio. Whatever was popular and mainstream, that was the stuff you would try to avoid like the plague."

Having seen the Hüskers show at the Paradise in Boston at which they performed 'Ticket To Ride' for an encore, Charles listened to them voraciously at home in his little flat. Of the half-dozen or so albums he had at the time, in fact, two were by the two-thirds gay Minnesotans. He played 'Green Eyes', from *Flip Your Wig*, over and over, along with Iggy's 'The Passenger'. At times, his poor Captain Beefheart tape wondered if it would ever glimpse the inside of his Walkman again.

They needed a name. Joey, who'd spent the first third of his life speaking Tagalog, and who was fascinated by English, proposed Pixies In Panoply after a presumably pleasurable prance through the dictionary's P pages. Panoply would soon be tossed on rock'n'roll history's scrapheap, where it nestled beside the Silver The Beatles had come to realise they didn't need. Amused by Iggy Pop and Billy Idol, Charles rechristened himself Black Francis, a choice he would never explain, though he would, when pestered by the press, reflexively offer something unfeasible about his dad's thwarted intention to give that name to the son he never had, or did have, but named something else.

If he was nothing else, it will, if it hasn't already, be seen, Charles was a smartass, and the advertisement he and Joey placed for a rhythm section in the *Boston Phoenix* wryly asserted that they wanted musicians who liked Hüsker Dü and Peter, Paul & Mary and had no chops. At the time, there probably weren't 25 Hüsker Dü fans in Boston who'd heard of Peter, Paul & Mary, and of those 25, 24 would almost certainly have regarded admitting a fondness for them as tantamount to having "I'm terminally unhip" tattooed on their foreheads, and would have concluded that the ad was some sort of cruel stitch-up. (Hadn't the *National Lampoon* started out, years before and just across the Charles [River], as the *Harvard Lampoon?*) But Mrs. John Murphy, the former Kim Deal, relocated to her husband's native Boston only a week before from her own native Ohio, was amused enough to be the advert's sole respondent.

Never mind that she didn't actually play bass, but guitar, and didn't actually have a bass with which to audition. Having grown up listening to people talking about corn and livestock, she could, after a fashion, sing harmony. In third grade, she'd drawn pentangles on her parents' porch, but later gave up witchcraft for music. She had a degree in biology, and was about to turn 25, but you wouldn't have known it from her speech, which was very much that of a teen ditz. She'd been a cheerleader (which is to say wholesome, an exemplar of the patriarchal notion of girls as decorative and subservient) in high school, but then a bit of a hellion, to the tune of once having been detained in a police holding cell, but could remember few of the juicy details, having been legless at the time. She'd first become interested in rock'n'roll after her twin sister Kelley came home from seeing the Led Zeppelin movie, *The Song Remains The Same*, on acid and told her what glorious fun being a rock star had looked.

After Kim got hold of a guitar and taught herself to play, she and twin sister Kelley played Blind Faith and Sam Cooke songs to bikers, once opening for the sad remnants of Steppenwolf, the 'Born To Be Wild' boys. Kelley graduated from college and moved to LA to work as a computer analyst, the idea being that Kim would soon join her. But Kim decided instead to marry John Murphy, to whom her brother had introduced her in Dayton – of which John Murphy had got bored within a few scant months of his company transferring him there. (When one is bored of Dayton, no one has ever observed, or is ever likely to, he is bored of life.)

Joey and Charles loved that Kim seemed to like Charles' stuff, and were relieved to have had a response to their ad, and wooed her with *hummus*. Hearing of her identical twin, Charles decided that Kelley should be the group's drummer. How could she prefer catering back in the Ohio outback to being part of a rock'n'roll band that was going to make it into a future edition of the *Rock Encyclopaedia*?

Charles lent Kim $50 towards bus fare back to said outback to borrow Kelley's bass guitar and change her mind.

Once having got back to Beantown with the instrument, but without her former wombmate, Kim and the two guitarists began rehearsing with a drum machine that kept exemplary time but wasn't much fun with whom to share a doobie. But then Kim remembered a fellow mentioning at her and John's wedding reception that he played the drums.

A lapsed electronic engineering student and John Murphy's former fellow employee at an electronics outlet store, local boy David Lovering loved the Canadian prog trio Rush, as most drummers did at the time, and metal-detecting, and had actually played in bands before. A seasoned professional! At 18, the drummer had visited a psychic who'd impressed him by divining not only his name and age, but also his interests in drumming and travel and even the name of his girlfriend. But when he asked if he had a future in music, she'd emphatically assured him he hadn't.

By the time the four of them first convened with their instruments, in a foetid rehearsal space on Boston's Kenmore Square, downstairs from a bar, in July 1986, Charles had already written the songs that would bring them their first fame. They began with 'Down To The Well' and worked that first day through nine or 10 more, including 'The Holiday Song', 'Caribou', and 'Here Comes Your Man', all destined to become Pixies classics, and a couple destined for little-noticed corners of bootleg albums, like 'Boom Chica Boom'. Joey thought the music too strange to get him out of the butcher block furniture warehouse for long, but it was a lot more fun than school. In the best rock'n'roll tradition (of the drummer joining last, and without fanfare), no one actually told Lovering that he was in. Instead, one of them wondered with a yawn if he might be interested in rehearsing with them again.

Only two months home from San Juan, Charles Thompson already had his band.

4

(Vicky's Story)
Chops

SOME girls wait forever to be asked out by anybody, even some-body with like oozing acne all over their face, and then are lucky if he decides to show up, and others just don't have enough evenings in a week to go out with all the majorly cute ones that ask. And I can promise you that those in the first group would like nothing more than to get their hands around the necks of those in the second and squeeze with all their might until they like ceased to struggle. When I got home pretty late from trying to console Tricia, Tiffani was still awake, pacing, wrestling with like a terrible dilemma. She'd already agreed to go out with this one guy Friday night, but then this other, much cuter one, had asked her too.

"Gosh, Tiff," I said, plopping onto the sofa, sitting on my hands to keep myself from doing something I might like regret, "I'd certainly hate to be in your shoes."

She gave my arm a little squeeze and looked at me soulfully with her like absurd huge eyes. "Thank you, Vicky." I originally thought it was stupidity that kept her from realising when I was being sarcas-tic – and I'm rarely anything else with her – but it probably isn't. I mean, she's premed. People like that, people who are good at like science, often don't have much to say about anything other than like biology or something, but that doesn't make them airheads.

And in Tiffani's case (when I saw the i at the end, I didn't even bother – there are some battles you just like know you're never going to win), she's got this major niceness thing going on. Girls as pretty as her (and I'm talking the whole nine yards – huge brown eyes, thick, glossy blonde hair, a to-die-for figure) are usually stuck-up little bitches, but she's like unnervingly nice, and to everybody, from the boys who are going to flunk out of premed because they can't concentrate around her, to old dears at bus stops, to the super of our building, who probably wouldn't be able to pick hers out of a pile of headshots, since all he ever looks at – stares at – are her boobs.

Like I said before, I don't think the two of us could have less in common. She's gorgeous and petite and saintly and Jewish (though she certainly doesn't look it), a majorly rich chiropractor's daughter from Brookline, and I'm the plain, overweight, cynical Anglo-American mongrel daughter of an unemployed alcoholic Southie. She only goes out on Friday nights because five of the other nights she's studying, and Saturday nights she volunteers at a homeless shelter. After helping serve dinner, she reads stories to whatever kids are there so their mums can have a couple of hours to themselves.

"The one guy, Grant," she tells me, "is in my biochemistry class. Don't get me wrong – he's a very sweet boy, very well-mannered and always perfectly groomed." Tiffani is probably the only girl in Cambridge who refers to guys as boys, and might be the only girl left in America who's interested in a guy's . . . grooming, whatever that means. "But Brad's a musician, and there's something kind of sexy about that, isn't there?"

Grant. Brad. Their names told you all you needed to know, didn't they? I could just picture them, Grant with his perfect grooming, almost certainly in a LaCoste shirt, and Brad, undoubtedly in a Christian rock group, although that's like a . . . what's it called . . . oxymoron. "Where'd you meet a musician?" I asked, wondering if poor Tricia had managed to get to sleep yet, imagining poor Dad snoring in front of the TV with an empty beer can on his belly.

"On the T. Last week. Last Saturday night. Coming home from volunteering. He had a guitar case. I normally don't speak with strangers on the T, but he was very well mannered, with a smile that just like disarmed me. It turned out we had a lot in common. He was on his way home from entertaining at an Alzheimer's care facility."

I waited for a punchline – prayed for one, in fact. But she wasn't joking.

Entertaining. Not singing. Not playing. Entertaining.

"Is that how he makes his living, entertaining Alzheimer's patients?"

She was like taken aback. "Oh, no, that's his good work. Completely unpaid, of course. He has a group that entertains in nightclubs. Oh, now I've forgotten what he said they were called. Something quite whimsical and funny."

I was tired enough to fall asleep right there on the sofa, but managed to get up. "Well, maybe the best thing is to like sleep on it," I yawned. "Maybe the answer about which one to go out with will like come to you in a dream or something."

"Yes," she said, not getting it again, "maybe. Listen, Vicky, before you go to bed, can we just chat for a second about privacy? The last couple of times I've had boys over, it's felt maybe just a little bit awkward with you, you know, staying out here in the living room."

She wasn't wrong. Our agreement – not that it ever actually applied to me – was that if one of us had a guy over, the other would keep like a low profile in her bedroom. I hadn't stayed in mine the last couple of times just to be a bitch, and because I frankly couldn't imagine why she needed privacy, since it was like inconceivable that she would let anybody touch her. But I was too tired to waste much more sarcasm on her. I told her I was sorry and would try not to forget again.

She decided on Brad in the end. (Poor Grant!) Girls like me and Tricia are ready and stewing in our own juices half an hour before the guy's even supposed to arrive to pick us up, but girls like Tiffani always need at least 15 more minutes. I didn't normally get a chance to talk to anybody as cute as Brad turned out to be for longer than a minute or two, so I tried to like make the most of his being stuck with me.

His band was called The Lamé Ducks – not lame, like stupid or feeble, but lamé, as in what Marc Bolan's stage clothing used to be made of, and that famous gold suit of Elvis'. I gathered they were kind of like Sha Na Na or something, kitsching up the Fifties, except they were apparently more about guitar rockers like Gene Vincent and Eddie Cochran than doo wop. They apparently made a ton of money. "People," Brad said, "just love that old stuff."

He also wrote songs of his own and hoped to put together a group to perform them. He was very into this English guy Richard Thompson I'd vaguely heard of but didn't know much about. Judging from the twinkle in Brad's eyes, my asking about his music pleased him.

I told him I liked The Ramones and Replacements and some old stuff like Talking Heads, but found Hüsker Dü a little bit too harsh for my taste. Talking Heads and The Ramones were the only ones he'd heard of. It occurred to me that no guy had ever thought to ask about my own tastes in music before. I certainly wasn't used to anybody so good-looking seeming to enjoy talking to me. I wished that Tiffani was having a fatal heart attack or something in her bedroom.

Brad asked if I played music. "Me?" I said, immediately feeling really stupid, since we were the only two people in the room. "No, when I was in primary school in London they asked if anybody was interested in learning, but there were a lot more kids wanting to learn than instruments. They lined us up and had us sing 'Land Of Hope And Glory' so they'd be able to see who had like aptitude, but when my turn came I was too shy, so I didn't get one." I was horrified to realise I might be babbling, but his eyes were still twinkling. I was pretty sure I was in love.

"A lot of really good musicians can't sing," he said. "But I suppose they had to do it one way or another. Haven't you ever wanted to learn to play the guitar?"

Well, I had. Of course I had. But I'd have felt pretty stupid admitting it.

"You might be too young to remember, but in around 1977 there were a lot of bands coming out of England who thought it might be fun to reverse the usual process and become rock stars before they actually learned to play. A lot of it was horrible, but some of it was pretty awesome, like The Clash." I did remember. It had always sounded to me, a primary school girl taller than all but two of the teachers at her school, as though their lead singer was like gargling with broken glass. "What that whole thing proved was that kids shouldn't feel they can't make their own music just because they haven't had like lessons and don't have chops. You ought to get hold of a guitar somewhere, Vicky, and see what you can come up with."

I nearly swooned. I think it was the first time a guy had ever like addressed me by name. It was such a stupid, common name, but it sounded like poetry coming out of Brad. I wanted to spend the rest of my life at his side. But here came Tiffani, looking so good that Brad actually said, "Oh, my," immediately making me feel really lumpish and huge and ugly. Oh, my. Like in some naff PG-rated movie or something.

Sitting home with my drunken dad and my little stepsister all those countless nights when I was in high school had sometimes hurt awfully, but if you'd somehow been able to add it all up, it wouldn't have compared to the hurt I felt as Brad and Tiffani left for their date, he touching the small of her back as they went out the door.

I had a good long cry, and then a beer. I phoned my dad's to find out if Tricia was doing OK, but all I got was the answering machine, which cut me off about two syllables into my message. My dad figured that no one would ever have anything good to tell him, so never answered the phone. The answering machine had been cutting callers off after a few syllables ever since I'd bought it for his birthday at a garage sale. Usually you couldn't even make out who'd called.

I turned on the TV. There was nothing that interested me. I got my Walkman and put in some Replacements. I wished I had some Richard Thompson. The guys in the apartment directly below played some interesting-sounding stuff sometimes (often when Tiffani was most intent on studying or I on sleeping). I thought of going down and asking if they had anything by him, but shyness kept me where I was.

I looked through the *Boston Phoenix* Tiffani had brought home. Naturally – there really is something to The Police's idea of synchronicity – it contained a review of Richard Thompson's *Daring Adventures*. Naturally. I read it through three times. If Brad ever brought him up again, I might not be able to speak from experience, but at least I'd be an expert on what the *Phoenix*'s writer thought, which I'd tell Brad is what I thought myself. The *Phoenix*'s writer thought Richard Thompson was God's gift to popular music, but that *Daring Adventures* wasn't up to his usual standard.

I pictured Brad and Tiffani looking gorgeous together and laughing at each other's jokes, showing their perfect white teeth (my own are so tiny that I try never to laugh with my mouth open around people). I nearly started crying again. There was still nothing on TV. I had some reading to do for class, but what sort of loser does school stuff on Friday night?

Just out of curiosity, I read some of the little musician classified adverts in the back of the *Phoenix*. I always fantasised about finding one that would ask for a big, bolshy virgin girl with no musical ability, but an English accent. As if. The members of Led Zeppelin could have had their pick of musical jobs in southern New England – nearly everybody was looking for other musicians "into Zeppelin" or at least "into Zep". But there was one that really stood out. It wanted a bass player and drummer into Hüsker Dü and Peter, Paul & Mary, without chops.

Up until an hour before, when Brad had used it, I'd never heard chops applied to anything other than cuts of lamb. If I'd understood him correctly, whoever had placed the advert was looking for someone kind of new to their instrument. Who could be newer than me, who'd never actually held a bass or a pair of drumsticks in their life? I was beginning to feel a bit better.

Hüsker Dü? Well, theirs wasn't the first tape I usually reached for, but I owned one, which was an awful lot more than most people could say, wasn't it? And Peter, Paul & Mary – that was obviously a joke. If I remembered correctly, they were like two geeky guys with like beatnik facial hair and a sexy blonde singer who did like really . . . earnest versions of Bob Dylan songs. It seemed to me that I'd seen them in one of those shows about Martin Luther King Jr. where everybody – regardless of colour! – joins hands at the end and stares soulfully at the camera while singing 'We Will Overcome', or whatever it was called.

It occurred to me that maybe I ought to give this some thought. If whoever had placed the ad were genuinely into that sort of thing, I wouldn't be doing myself any favours making like overt fun of it. I decided what I'd say, if they asked me if I really liked them, is, "Well, who doesn't?" with my eyebrow like arched so I'd be able to claim I was stitching them up if it turned out they were just being coy. Irony on top of irony!

I rang the number. There was loud music playing in the background. The guy who answered sounded pretty well baked. When I told him I was responding to his advert in the *Phoenix*, he was confused at first, and then fairly excited. He put his hand over the receiver, but not completely, so I was able to hear him holler over the music, "Dude, somebody's calling about the ad!" It suddenly occurred to me while I waited for him to come back that I ought to get at least a little familiar with an instrument before I met these guys. Which meant I'd have to figure out where to rent instruments and everything! Why hadn't I thought this through before making the call?

"So when do you want to audition?" the guy asked. I told him I was going to be . . . out of town. I wondered if two weeks was OK. I considered telling him I was going to be on tour, but of course people who went on tour had chops, so that wouldn't work.

"Two weeks is awesome," he agreed. "That'll give us time to get a few more songs together."

"Cool," I said, "I'll call you when I get back in town."

"Cool," he said.

I couldn't remember when I'd felt so excited and happy. I went into the bathroom with my Walkman and pretended to be playing bass with The Replacements. I wondered if wearing your bass really, really low to the ground, like Dee Dee in The Ramones, made it harder to play. I know it looked really cool. If that girl in Talking Heads could do it, and the Sonic Youth one, why couldn't I?

Tiffani wasn't thrilled to find me in the living room when she and Brad got back from wherever they'd been. You could see it in her eyes. But my asking Brad if he'd show me how to play bass wouldn't wait.

"Well, I'd be pleased to," he said, "next time I'm over." He looked at Tiffani, apparently for like verification that there'd be a next time, but she was looking at me, glaring, kind of, or at least as close to it as she gets.

"Cool!" I said, "but this is kind of urgent. I thought maybe I could come early to one of your band's rehearsals or something."

"Sure," he said, picking up on Tiffani's impatience. "We'll do that. I'll get Tiff to give you my number. You can call me tomorrow or something."

"Awesome," I said. "Is there anything I can do to like prepare?"

Tiffani sighed in annoyance. I was testing her saintliness to the max . . .Tiff's.

"Nothing comes to mind," Brad said. "Maybe learn to count the beats in a bar or something? The bass typically plays with the kick drum, on one and three."

"Can you run that by me again, in English this time?"

Brad put his hand to his face, trying to like conceal that he was smirking. And poor Tiffani – talk about somebody wanting to get their hands around somebody's throat and squeeze until you cease to struggle! "I just remembered a lot of reading I have to get done this weekend," I said, and finally left them alone. I went back in my room and listened to The Replacements on my Walkman, trying to figure which was the bass guitar and which the real ones.

The Lamés rehearsed in the back of a lace warehouse in Southie. I was there nearly an hour early, well before the first of them – the drummer – turned up. He was a lot older than Brad, and not cute, and not friendly. He kept his cigarette in the corner of his mouth while he did a bunch of boring exercises, losing his ash onto his snare drum a couple of times. Then Brad showed up. Since the bass player wasn't there, we'd have to use his guitar instead, just what we called the bottom four strings, even though it looked to me like they were on top. The minute I had the guitar strapped on, I felt like a new person. He plugged the guitar into an amplifier. I can't begin to describe how powerful it made me feel.

He said he'd show me a walking bass line for a blues in A. I didn't want to seem ungrateful, but I didn't want him to waste his time either, so I told him I wasn't very interested in the blues. He laughed and said that's just what like a standard rock'n'roll chord progression was called. He got behind me and reached around me to play. The drummer tapped along. I was getting a little wet.

I tried it. It was around a million times harder than Brad had made it seem. I didn't even start in the right place, on the right fret. Brad was really sweet and patient, though. He said maybe we were trying to run before we could walk, and that probably he should just teach me to play the tonic for the chords in a blues in A. I thought tonic was a sort of water. What he showed me this time was certainly a lot easier, but I still found it really hard to remember which string to play, and which fret.

I wondered if maybe I'd be better off learning to play the drums, which wouldn't require me to know the names of all the different notes. The drummer made a big show of jumping right up off his little stool and handing me his sticks. "Hey, go for it," he said. I gathered he thought I was saying that anybody could play the drums.

I sat down on his little stool and tapped a couple of things, a drum and a cymbal. I'd have bet the drummer would have been a lot more helpful if I'd been petite and in spandex. Brad began strumming his guitar, but I didn't come in. "I'm not really sure what I'm supposed to do," I admitted when he finally stopped. I thought my face must have been about the colour of the B on the Red Sox cap. It was like total humiliation.

The drummer rolled his eyes. Wanker. He motioned for me to get up and said to watch carefully. Brad began to play again. The drummer counted out loud. First he started playing the big drum on the floor with one of his foot pedals, and then the snare. I could see that you never played them at the same time. This was obviously going to be a lot easier. Then he began stepping on the high hat with his left foot at the same time he was hitting the snare drum with his left hand. Finally, he began tapping one of his cymbals steadily. I thought I was beginning to get it, but he got up off his stool again before I felt really comfortable with the whole idea.

Brad started playing. I played the big drum on the floor, the kick drum, as the drummer called it. It sounded really good! Brad was nodding at me! This was going to work! But then I tried to get my right hand working at the same time as my right foot, and the whole thing fell apart big time.

"This time," the drummer said, "try starting off with eighth notes with the right hand before you add everything else in." He nodded at the big cymbal and pantomimed playing it. It sounded good. Brad looked pleased. But then I tried to add the kick drum, and the wheels came off the cart again, just as another member of the group showed up. It was pretty clear they all wanted to talk to each other before rehearsal began, so I got up and told Brad I'd practise what I learned at home, and got out of there quick.

Maybe it was that Brad, however sweet, was hard to play along with. Maybe he'd been doing something that required like a more sophisticated approach or something. I went back to my apartment and put my headphones on, figuring I didn't need real drums to practise. I tapped my thigh with my right hand as though it was the ride cymbal, and tapped my foot, as though pressing the kick drum pedal down, but it just wasn't working. I could never get more than two of four working together. If I started with my feet, everything would fall apart when I tried to add one of my hands. If I started with my hands, I couldn't add my feet.

Maybe it was The Replacements. Maybe that was it. I looked through Tiffani's tapes and found one by Debbie bloody Gibson, the most wholesome girl in America. I figured if anything would be easy, it would be Debbie Gibson music. God, I hoped so.

Same thing. It didn't seem to matter who I tried to play along with. I didn't begin to see how anybody did it. I would never have a bad syllable to say about the drummer in even the lamest group again. I could only hope that the baked-sounding guy on the phone was able to find somebody else into Hüsker Dü and Peter, Paul & Mary, though I doubt that he could have found anybody with less chops.

5

A Thumb-Sized Cock

THE new band took to rehearsing five nights a week, either, depending on whose reminiscence you embrace, in the fetid Kenmore Square basement – with its sewer cap in the middle of the room, its nearly unendurable stench, its fleas and insects – or, rather less romantically, in Lovering's father's garage. They played no covers. Even with Joey's weird system of tablature, Charles' was really the only music they could play, its occasional bizarre time signatures notwithstanding. "The weirder the time signature is," Charles would claim years hence, "the less conscious I am of it, actually. Maybe it's because I really don't know what I'm doing is wrong or right. It's the way I hear it – the advantage of being untrained as a musician, I guess."

When they came up with their big trick of playing the verses quietly and the choruses as though trying to liquefy the walls with sheer volume, it seemed a fairly obvious ploy to them, no big deal at all. And when rehearsal was done, they hung out with one another, and enjoyed one another's company. No one had been able to figure Joey out yet, but that hadn't stopped Kim from lending him her Les Paul gold-top guitar – exactly what the doctor ordered in view of Charles having made quite clear that there was room in the band for only one Telecaster man, himself, even if he did seem to play acoustic on most songs. Delighted to be making music, Charles was keen and buoyant, but Lovering alone dared predict that they were destined for the toppermost of the poppermost. One day, he said, the Rat would be a distant memory, and they'd play the Orpheum Theater, Beantown's most prestigious venue.

Strangely, his recollection of their first public appearance is that it was at the Rathskellar, widely perceived as Beantown's answer to the Bowery's CBGBs, and that those of their friends who turned up found them hilariously awful. It is elsewhere recorded, though, that their debut, for which they were paid $17 and referred to in a print ad as The Puxies, was actually at Jack's on Mass Ave. in Cambridge, which would burn down seven months later in mysterious circumstances – because of the proprietor's desire to reap a large insurance settlement? – and that the small audience loved them almost from Charles' first scream.

He screamed, he would later explain, because he wanted to rivet the audience's attention (though he would later become notorious for seemingly ignoring the audience), and didn't feel that wiggling his bum was likely to do the trick. "You're constantly trying to draw attention to yourself or to the song by stopping it and starting it again. You have to make it interesting, to entertain, and I don't know how to do it, so it's the easiest way. Just start hacking away at things. Mixing it all up."

They played a strip joint in Lowell, to an audience comprising more tipsy middle-aged lechers than college kids, and were deeply gratified by their warm reception. "It's more a compliment," Charles would later observe, "for someone who doesn't listen to rock music to say, 'Hey, I don't know what it is, but I liked it.'" A girl with large breasts asked if she could manage them, pleasing Joey, and they soon found themselves playing Tuesday nights at the Rat, just as The Who, two decades before, had played the Marquee in Soho. A poster depicting a naked Charles in a semi-foetal position with one of his thumbs appearing to be his cock attracted considerable local attention, as how could it not? If Charles was horrified to imagine that he was perceived as having a thumb-sized cock, he kept it to himself. They accepted the opening slot on a Rat bill featuring Big Dipper and Throwing Muses.

Fresh from having discovered Throwing Muses, producing their first recordings, and consequently being applauded in the hippest places for it, Gary Smith – whose own group, Lifeboat, had already sprung a fatal leak, ha ha, and would soon sink – dropped by the Rat one early evening in November 1986 to commune with his protégés as the Pixies were conducting their sound check.

He couldn't believe what he saw and heard. The bass player was a girl, and given to a winsome smirk that could have melted the heart of Milosevic, but there was nothing earth-shattering about the rhythm section. The two guitar players, though, were another story entirely! The swarthy one – Mexican? Other Hispanic? – seemed to have learned to play on Mars, or by listening over and over to Jeff Beck's imitations of barnyard animals in 'I Ain't Superstitious'. But it was the singer, fair-haired, fresh-faced, every inch a clean-cut American kid, who took the cake. One second he'd be singing in a pleasant first tenor that would have been right at home with 'Leavin' On A Jet Plane'. The next he was screaming as though he hated that bitch – in Spanish. And then, in another song, everything stopped for a moment so he could mumble, "You are the son of a motherfucker".

"Jesus, Mary, and Joseph," Smith, apparently the beneficiary of a parochial education, has remembered thinking to himself, "I've got to get a piece of this!"

There are groups that are fantastic in the rehearsal room and at sound checks, but who freeze up when paying punters are watching. The Pixies proved not to be one of them, and Smith, who watched open-mouthed from right in front of the stage, could hardly wait for the show to end so he could hurry backstage to inform the Pixies that he wanted desperately to record them, to write his phone number on a serviette and give it to Charles. Already accustomed to the adoration of strangers, the group didn't jump up and down with glee at the idea, but didn't seem offended by it either.

Smith and Charles conferred a couple of times on the phone and over breakfast. What Smith proposed was that Charles let him record the group at Fort Apache. A quartet of local musicians turned producers and engineers, hereinafter the Roxbury Four, had opened the Fort early the year before as a joint venture. They included Joseph Incagnoli, better known as Joe Harvard, formerly Harvard University's reigning punk maven and the singer and guitarist of such notable local bands as the bones, and Sean Slade, formerly Yale University's punk maven and a member, with the remaining two, Jim Fitting and Paul Kolderie, of The Sex Execs. The four shared a passion for adventurous new music of the sort Mitch Easter and Don Dixon were recording in informal settings down South with groups like R.E.M., but had been able to raise only around $9,000 between them, and so had built their studio in part of the gigantic commercial laundry building at 169 Norfolk Street, Roxbury, a neck of the woods in which only the brave or foolish ventured after dark, and in which no unattended parked car went unvandalised for more than a few minutes. Joe came out one night to find his truck flipped over and burning in the street. Slade's car was stolen. Every window of Kolderie's was smashed, and his stereo ripped out.

In this age of being able to produce quite credible recordings on an iBook, one might lack perspective on what a crucial sea change studios like Fort Apache represented. Not long before, most groups could only dream of being able to get themselves viably recorded, as most studios were inconceivably expensive, geared to coke-addled superstars who'd book them for a month at a time and then, while their coke-addled record company patrons dutifully wrote out cheques, sit around sniffling and waiting for inspiration.

It was all very circular. If you played most music biz movers and shakers a demonstration tape recorded on anything less than state-of-the-art gear, they'd tell you, "Hey (music biz movers and shakers invariably began their sentences with hey), it sounds a little . . . unfinished." But to be able to afford to get into a studio capable of producing something that would sound finished, you'd need record company bucks galore. So the rich got richer (and thus able to afford even more toot), and the poor stayed poor. And it was the audience that suffered most, having to content itself with the well-recorded, seldom inspired, music of cocaine-addled superstars.

Along with The Turbines, The Neat, and Treat Her Right, whose ultra-low-budget recording RCA would license, and from which Morphine mainstay Marc Sandman would later emerge, Fort Apache's early clients had included Lifeboat, for which Smith played 12-string guitar, wrote songs, often with political themes, and sang. His pitch to the Pixies was as follows. If the group could scrape together a nominal pile of cash, he, entitled to some gratis hours by virtue of having signed on to manage the studio, would record them in it.

Lifeboat embarked on its final tour. Smith sent Charles a postcard from Nowheresville, or wherever it was, asserting that he wouldn't rest until the Pixies were world-famous. Having determined that his parents would lend him the $1,000 Fort Apache asked, Charles was sufficiently impressed to go over, when Lifeboat got home to Boston, to Smith's apartment to sing several of the songs the band might wish to record. Smith had earlier recorded other songwriters in this way, as part of what he enjoyed thinking of as his Sing-for-Your-Supper series. With nothing but his acoustic guitar, Charles somehow was able to convey that the verses would be subdued and the choruses orgasmic, volcanic, apocalyptic.

En route to a Muses gig the following week, Smith played Charles' Sing-for-Your-Supper tape for a British journalist despatched to America to find out all about Throwing Muses, and the guy was suitably awe-struck, as too was his other passenger, the lapsed psychotherapist turned Muses manager Ken Goes.

A fortnight and change later, the Pixies were in the studio – and in the studio, and in the studio, and in the studio, for three days and nights on the trot. They'd start with a rhythm track – bass, drums, and both Charles and Joey playing rhythm – and then overdub lead and acoustic guitars, percussion, and all the vocals, the latter in the cavernous, wooden-floored, empty warehouse space outside the studio proper. Loathing the sound of synthetic reverb, Smith had Paul Kolderie, acting as engineer, set up three mikes, one into which Kim or Charles would sing, and two, at a considerable remove, for ambience. At one point Joey, not one to stand on ceremony, tried to enjoy a wee nap on the wooden floor, only to be awakened – as rudely as it's possible to be awakened – by the sound of Charles, his features contorted into a mask of unutterable anguish or rage, screaming as though he hated that bitch.

"The first Pixies album?" Kolderie has reminisced. "If you can picture it, Black Francis is out there in the middle of this room as big as a football field, with one fluorescent bulb flickering, and he's just kind of going, 'Arrrrgh!'"

Charles was still trying to polish off the lyrics for 'Levitate Me' when it was time to record his lead vocal, and was turning down no reasonable suggestions, one of which came from David Lovering, another from someone called Walsh. But when Smith hit Record, Charles seemed to have had the song deep in his genes from the moment of his conception, seemed to know it as intimately as a 68-

year-old church lady in, well, Dayton knows 'What A Friend We Have In Jesus'. As Smith stood there with the other Pixies in the dark control room, he knew he'd done the right thing betting his complimentary hours on this fresh-faced blond kid and his crew.

Everyone went home for a week and then reconvened to mix down what they'd recorded, in another marathon session. Disaster struck as the punch-drunk Smith rewound the two-track tape onto which they were mixing down too far and recorded over the end of 'Vamos'. He phoned poor Kolderie at six in the morning to appeal to him to come and help.

Poor David Lovering had been photographed cavorting naked at Fort Apache (sleep deprivation inspires even the most inhibited to behave peculiarly) during one of the group's endless sessions. The photograph found its way, beneath big purple letters, onto the cassette insert the group had designed. A couple of hundred copies of the tape were run off. It was offered for sale at Newbury Comics, Boston's hippest record store, and sent to a few select movers and shakers, all of whom turned it down.

By this time, the Pixies had urged their original manager to take her ample décolletage elsewhere, and were being managed by Ken Goes, who had ample reason to trust Gary Smith's recommendation. When Ivo Watts-Russell, the visionary founder of 4AD, the label that released the Muses' music in Britain, visited Rhode Island to commune with the Muses, who lived there (and were driven up to gigs from there by a dad with a station wagon), Goes played him *The Purple Tape*.

He wasn't, to resort to the hyperbolic parlance of the music biz, blown away. It was Mrs. John Murphy's belief that he found it too American, which is to say too loud and obnoxious, for his 4AD label, whose stock in trade was artfully packaged (the label had a crackerjack in-house design team in 23 Envelope) melancholia. Ivo had founded his label, whose most notable stars would include Bauhaus, The Birthday Party, and the sublime Cocteau Twins, in 1980 with the idea of making it a home to music not easily categorised – though there were those who believed that an awful lot of it was pretty easily categorised as Goth.

His girlfriend, the brave little label's publicist – and Ivo's love interest – thought the Pixies fab, though, and prevailed on him to reconsider. He did so, and offered to issue in Britain a sort of mini-album comprising his eight favourite tracks from *The Purple Tape*. Pleased by Gocs' assurance that 4AD paid punctually, and loving the idea of "having" to perform abroad, the Pixies eagerly agreed to join Ivo's roster.

He named the disk *Come On Pilgrim*, without a comma, after the Larry Norman exhortation Charles had slipped quietly into 'Levitate Me' because it put him in mind of Billy Pilgrim, hero of Kurt Vonnegut's *Slaughterhouse-Five*.

Charles and his girlfriend – his honey, as he preferred it – lay side by side listening to the record shortly before its release while most of the rest of Beantown slumbered. "You're special," Jean marvelled when it was finished. "You're different. You've done a really good job here."

6

(Vicky's Story)
Delusions of Mattering

A FEW months after the beginning and ending of my career as a musician, Tiffani was still "seeing" Brad. It sounded so like genteel or something when she put it that way it like made my flesh crawl. Of course most of the stuff she did had come to make my flesh crawl. Every time Brad would see me, he'd say, "So how's the drumming coming?" which I guess he thought really clever because it rhymed. The first few times he asked, I said fine because I didn't want to get in some big like rah-rah talk with him about how all I needed was enough determination. I was satisfied that all the determination in the world wasn't going to make a musician of me, and that my like rightful place was watching bands, and not playing in them. The next time he asked me, I said, "I've given them up for the violin." He gaped like delightedly and said, "Hey, that's terrific, Vicky. The violin!" He didn't know when his leg was being pulled anymore than Her Perfectness, which I'd come to call Tiffani now, but not to her face.

A couple of weeks after I found the Debbie Gibson tape in her collection, I asked her about it. I'd been afraid she might accuse me of snooping through her like personal stuff is why it took me so long. But when I asked her if she might be willing to let me borrow it, she just gave me this like offended (because I thought I needed to ask?) look, and said, "Of course you can! Isn't that album just the coolest?" I kind of hated myself for making fun of her. It was like small consolation that she had no idea I was even doing it.

I decided what I'd do to compensate was take her to hear my favourite new local band. I'd been going over to Boston a lot the past few weeks to see bands at this club called the Rathskellar. It was like majorly seedy, but the atmosphere was really exciting. Being in the audience there made you feel like you were discovering something like really special, something people like Tiffani didn't know anything about. Some of the bands sucked big time, but others, like Big Dipper and Treat Her Right (and was that the coolest name for a band anybody had ever thought of?) were so good they made me wet. My own favourite was Lifeboat. They had two guitar players, one of them on a 12-string, and they had really good songs. They didn't try too hard to be weird, like a lot of bands you saw there did. You could hum some of their stuff.

Brad was supposed to be a musician, but he looked almost as uncomfortable as Tiff when we went in. "Well," she said, trying to sound like cheerful, "it's certainly like no nightclub I've ever been in before."

"Me neither," Brad agreed. "But it doesn't smell all that different from some men's rooms I've been in." I was glad to see he was smiling when he said that.

Even I thought the very punky first band, whose name I didn't catch, and didn't particularly want to catch, sucked, though I pretended to think they were really awesome so Her Perf and Brad wouldn't insist on going. I noticed that Tiff was getting a lot of attention. People weren't used to seeing anybody so clean-cut there. The guys weren't used to seeing anybody that good-looking.

"Now you can't tell me, Vicky," Brad said when the punky first band finally shut up, "that it would take you longer than a couple of weeks to play at least as well as those clowns." It had seemed to me that the drummer was really good.

Before Lifeboat came on, I got Brad and Her Perf to push up toward the front with me. "You've got to get the whole experience," I said. Her Perf made her cutest like dubious face, but they followed me. It was like the Red Sea parting for us or something. I don't think anybody wanted to take a chance of smudging Her Perf's immaculate white jumper by brushing against it.

When Lifeboat started their set, it actually was pretty loud, and she stuck her fingers in her ears with another like adorable expression, but she was a good sport, and took them out after the first song. The band were really good, and by the fourth song, she and Brad both seemed to be enjoying themselves. My own favourite moment was when the 12-string guitarist smiled at me – and there was no like mistaking it was me he was smiling at – while the other guitar player did a little solo. Nothing like that had ever happened to me before.

On the way home, Her Perf amused Brad by pretending not to be able to hear him. Normally I'd have found that like majorly annoying, but I was too busy remembering the 12-string guitar dude's smile.

When I saw him the next week (not in Tiffani sense of like dating him, but literally) at a coffee shop in Harvard Square, I nearly like hyperventilated or something. He was sitting there by himself, sipping some coffee, occasionally glancing out the window, but mostly reading the *Phoenix*. I sat down in a booth of my own hoping he'd notice. He looked in my direction at one point, but didn't seem to recognise me. I thought of a million things I could go over and say to him, but they'd all come to seem totally stupid within a second or two of like conception. I didn't think I'd be able to bear it if he just like glared at me or something. He was probably pretty used to girls trying to like talk to him.

I figured maybe I'd better just forget it. And then felt like a total wuss for thinking that. Nothing ventured, nothing gained. Survival of the fittest. Would he embarrass me worse than the other girls at my junior high school had done more times than I could count, or boys?

I made myself walk over. He looked up from his paper and said, "Hi." He didn't recognise me. He looked at me like quizzically. I'd used up all my like resolve or whatever just getting myself over there. I couldn't make a sound! But then I finally did. I told him I'd been at the Rat the other night, and seen his band play, and really liked it. I managed to stop myself before asking if he remembered smiling at me.

He was really like cordial. He said, "Well, that's very kind of you. I appreciate that very much . . .", waiting for me to tell him my name. One of my favourite local musicians wanted to know my name! He told me his name was Gary, and shook my hand, putting his left one on top of mine in the way that like really warm people do. He asked if I wanted to sit down. They hadn't invented the drug that could make somebody feel what I was feeling!

He told me his band was just on the verge of playing its last show ever. They'd stopped getting along. I was so excited and proud to be sitting there with him that he could have told me my dad had a like inoperable brain tumour and it wouldn't have fazed me. I was right in the middle of trying to decide how to ask him what he planned next without sounding really stupid when this little round blond guy presented himself. "Hey!" Gary said, really excitedly. They shook hands soul-style.

"This is Charles," Gary said, as Charles slid into the booth beside me. "He's got a band of his own, and they're phenomenal." So here I, Vicky Tighe, the girl too big and bolshy for anybody at East Boston High School other than the likes of Cory and Ryan to ask out, was just casually hanging out with two like way notable (I was willing to take Gary's word about Charles) local rock musicians, listening to them make plans for Charles to come over to Gary's house to play him some songs. Oh, I thought, I could really get to like this.

I was willing to take Gary's word about anything.

But it was too good to last. A tall, really pretty redhead with blue eyes nearly the size of Her Perf's and even bigger boobs was suddenly there with us, leaning over to kiss Gary hello on the lips. He greeted her as "babe". He said, "You and Charles already know each other, babe. And this is . . . I'm sorry. Was it Valerie?"

No, it wasn't. And there went my like delusions of mattering to these people. And it was pretty clear from the look Babe gave me as she slid in beside Gary that she wouldn't mind if I remembered urgent business elsewhere. Which was at least a little flattering – a girl who looked like her thinking of big bolshy Vicky Tighe from Eastie as competition!

"Well," I said, getting up, "places to see, people to go." It wasn't until it was out of my mouth that I realised I'd like jumbled the expression up, but Gary, bless his heart, seemed to think I'd done it on purpose. "Hey, I like that," he said, "don't you, babe?" And Babe gave me an even dirtier look than before. I like cherished the memory of it all the way out to Jeffries Point to see my dad and stepsister.

My dad was asleep and Tricia, who'd taken to like putting on airs, was wearing sunglasses indoors.

My dad hadn't had a drink in like three days, she said, but he'd hardly got out of bed either. He'd been sleeping 20 hours a day. She'd gone in to check on him and to feel his forehead to make sure he wasn't like on fire with fever or something, but he hadn't seemed feverish.

I went into his room. If Brad hadn't liked the smell of the Rat, God knows what he'd have had to say about this! You had to breathe through your mouth. He was asleep on the eighth of his bed nearest the open window, all tangled up in a single sheet, naked except for a pair of briefs I wished I hadn't seen, all full of stains and holes. He usually shaved himself at least a few times a week. It was like his sole concession to the idea of good grooming. But judging from the ugly bristly white whiskers all over his face and throat, it had been several days since he'd managed it. The whiskers didn't match what remained of his hair, which he dyed black. He'd drooled out of the corner of his mouth, and it had just dried there. I went into the bathroom to get a washcloth to clean it off. He woke up enough to mumble, "Yo, Vic." It broke my heart.

"Catching up on our beauty sleep, are we?" I teased him with a lump in my throat.

"Yeah, I guess you could say that. My beauty sleep. You might laugh, but it was me the chicks chased in the Lids days – me, me and the drummer. I don't remember his name just now." He began to cry, so softly at first that I didn't know it was happening, and then sobbing big time. I breathed through my mouth and held him.

"How do you suppose I feel," he sobbed, "not even being able to defend her? Well, I'll tell you how. Like the lowest speck of shit on the face of the earth."

"Defend who?" I said.

"Leave me alone now," he said, struggling with the hopelessly tangled sheet, trying in vain to pull it up over himself. "I'm too tired to talk about it anymore today."

I went back out to Tricia and asked if she knew what he was on about. She said she'd rather not talk about it. "Well, you fucking *are* going to talk about it," I said, stepping between her and the TV. "Count on it." I reached behind me and turned the TV off.

"Why do you always have to get your fucking way?" she howled. It was twice now I'd heard her swear. She slipped off her sunglasses to reveal an ugly black eye, and then replaced them. "Are you happy now?" she said. "Turn it back on, OK?"

I stood my ground.

"Fuck," she said. "Fuck, fuck, fuck. Jesus. Why does everything have to be so like complicated all the time?"

I stood my ground.

"I've been seeing somebody," she said, "OK? He's like my boy-friend. I didn't want you to like find out because I know you're like hypersensitive about guys not liking you. But now you know, OK?"

It didn't seem like the time or place to tell her about how the girl-friend of a cool local rock star had seemed to think of me as competi-tion. "Somebody from school?" I asked.

"Oh, yeah, right. Like I'd take a chance agreeing to go out with another of those losers. After the first one didn't show up and didn't even call. I'm so sure. No, Dennis is older, more mature."

"How much older, Tricia?"

"God, why is everybody so fucking hung up on numbers?"

"How much older, Tricia?"

"He's 26."

"And you don't think that might be a little old for you?"

"You're just jealous, Vicky. Do you think I can't see how jealous you are because I already have a boyfriend at 17 and you've barely gone out on a fucking date at almost 20?"

I don't know how, but I found the strength not to react to that, and it worked like a charm. She ran over and threw her arms around me. "It's not like anybody my own age has any interest in me, is it?" she sobbed. "Dennis makes me feel like really desirable."

I guided her back to the sofa. We sat down together. I put my arm around her. She stopped sobbing after a while and told me some of the details. Her best girlfriend Cari had an after-school and weekend job as a waitress at the convalescent hospital where Dennis was one of the cooks. After Tricia visited Cari there one afternoon, Dennis got Cari to give him Tricia's phone number. He asked her out. He took her to a really nice dinner at Sizzler. It was the first time she'd ever had lobster.

As I asked if they'd got like . . . intimate, I wondered if sex education teachers felt as stupid putting it that way as I did. Tricia wanted to know how that was any of my business.

"It's my business as your stepsister if you get knocked up and have to drop out of school and your whole life gets screwed up, isn't it?"

She changed the subject. "There was a guy at the restaurant smiling at me, looking at my legs. I wore a short skirt." When the guy got up to leave, Dennis like excused himself and followed him out into the parking lot. I could see through the window. He twisted the guy's arm up behind his back and pushed his face down on the hood of his car. His nose was bleeding."

"I don't understand why you want me to know that, Tricia. What does that tell us?"

"That he's going to protect me! Do you really not see that?"

"From guys looking at your legs when you wear short skirts? How about if you don't wear short skirts in the first place? And you haven't told me about your eye."

"We've been out four times now," she said. "He took me to his favourite bar. (Me and Cari got fake ID from this guy up in Revere a couple of months ago.) I wore my short skirt again. He said not to, but I thought he was just saying that. He's told me how much he likes my legs. There were these two guys at the bar talking about them, I guess. Dennis heard them say they'd like to have them wrapped around their backs or something. He went over and asked them to come outside with him. They were like intimidated and wouldn't do it. One of them complained to like the bar manager, and we were asked to leave.

"Dennis didn't say anything until we got back to his place. When he called me a little cockteaser, I slapped him. He hit me. In the eye. It was all a misunderstanding."

"A misunderstanding! Fuckin'-A it was a misunderstanding! Your going out with somebody who picks fights with strangers in bars, with somebody who hits women, is one like mega-misunderstanding if you ask me, Tricia. Jesus. You give me his phone number. I'm going to have a word with him."

"You couldn't get it out of me with a fucking team of horses, Vicky," she said, sneering. "Do you really think I'm going to let you screw everything up for me?"

"Me and Tiffani have the fucking Yellow Pages, Tricia. If I have to, I'll phone every convalescent hospital in Greater Boston until I find one that has a cook called Dennis. I swear to God I will!"

There was panic in her eyes. All of a sudden, she looked around 12. "Please don't, Vic. Please! Do you know how much respect I'm getting at school now it's got around that I've got an older boyfriend? It's like my status has gone through the ceiling. Vicky, please, please, please don't do it."

"I see one more mark on you," I said, "your team of bloody horses won't be able to stop me."

7

One of Those Indie Bands

THE gorgeous, disturbing cover 23 Envelope designed for *Pilgrim* bore no trace of the Pixies, but depicted some poor devil with hair on his back so thick you could have hidden dimes in it. There was no mention of Charles Thompson, but rather of Black Francis. La Deal, as though trapped in some terrifying dream of the Fifties, was credited as Mrs. John Murphy.

Though none described the band as poetically and perceptively as Michael Azerrad would years later when he called them "a roiling amalgam of X, Neil Young and primal-scream therapist Arthur Janov" offering a "grinding, shrieking slab of guitar hell", no few Brits, many of them with typewriters, praised them feverishly.

"These tales of dark lands and deeds," *NME* marvelled, "are illuminated by smiling tunes veined with quicksilver flashes of guitar. It's this sleight-of-hand, together with a morbid humour which surfaces slowly upon repeated plays, that makes Pixies so addictive." *Sounds* mused, "Have they excavated some dark and ancient secret that might possibly require careful handling, or have they simply rediscovered good old-fashioned rock'n'roll, spicing it up with dazzling splashes of individuality to give their find an impression of freshness? The answer is probably a bit of both." *Q* felt sure it detected "hints of Patti Smith's brash poetry, while the wild anxiousness of Iggy Pop floats around on the backs of equally nervous guitars. In other words, the Pixies project a harsh and tense post punk rock experience that loves to trade insults." The disc reached the Top 5 in the UK indie charts, meaning that it must have sold well over 100 copies, and yes, cheap shot.

Hardly 18 months home from Rio Piedras, and Charles M.K. Thompson IV, unmistakably fortune's fair-haired boy, had a band that was being praised and selling well in the land that had given us The Beatles, the Stones and The Who. It all seemed somehow . . . ordained. It was nearly embarrassing!

But of course it made other Boston bands, with whom the Pixies had next to nothing to do extracurricularly, jealous and resentful. Didn't they understand that you were supposed to spend a couple of years breathing cigarette smoke and beer fumes in scuzzy clubs and go through a couple of million personnel upheavals before you signed with a local label like Taang or Ace of Hearts, your good showing on which might get you an offer for your next record from a national indie like Black Flag's SST or Touch and Go? Who exactly did Charles and his little mob, only one of whom was an actual homeboy, think they were?

If that made Charles repentant, he kept it well hidden. A couple of years hence, he would assure an interrogator, "We never had anything to do with [the Boston scene], not in the smallest way. We just ended up there, made some demos, and got out as soon as we could." To another, he would reveal himself to be Mr. Nose-to-the-Grindstone: "I remember practising in the rehearsal space five or six nights a week, spending like $400 a month for this shithole to rehearse in. I remember going down there and never seeing any other bands rehearse. On the weekends they'd be down there partying, so I felt good when we were rehearsing. I felt like we were the only band actually rehearsing."

The lapsed psychotherapist Ken Goes, meanwhile, began acting as though he were Albert Grossman or somebody, treating Gary Smith, without whom none of it might have happened, like dirt. Gary's deal with the band had been that he would receive two per cent of their take if the music they'd recorded was ever released. It was Goes' view, though, that one per cent was sufficiently generous.

Smith and Joe Harvard believed the Pixies to be definitively booked into Fort Apache for a few weeks for their first recording since the release of *Come On Pilgrim*, but Goes seemed to think the booking wasn't so definitive at all. Ten days before it was to begin, he phoned poor Joe, largely through whose largesse *Pilgrim* had been recorded in the first place, asserting that they needed to agree on a price, although Harvard had quoted him one before the booking. Goes now wanted a *better* price. Never mind that such clients of the studio as Big Dipper, about to begin their third album there, were content to pay the going rate.

Incensed, Harvard decided to leave it up to Gary Smith, who, when he heard what Goes was up to, was fit to be tied. Goes wound up booking the Pixies into a rival studio, Q-Division, compelling Fort Apache to scramble frantically to try to fill the hours they'd had booked. Joe Harvard liked to imagine that Charles was mortified with embarrassment when he found out, but as of spring 2004, Ken Goes was still his manager.

The Pixies got an offer of help – specifically, vocal – from an Emerson College girl, a Filipino doctor's daughter from Woon-socket, Rhode Island. In spite of her impressive credentials – she'd toured with the ferociously wholesome Up With People and com-posed a jingle for Digital Equipment Corporation – Joey pointed out to her that they already had a girl backup singer in Mrs. John Murphy. But she would be heard from again.

Rather than come over to Britain to cash in, the band ventured out into the hinterlands, onto the roach-infested motel circuit. They were seen in Kalamazoo. They were seen in Kansas. They played and played and played, and drove and drove and drove. It all seemed a marvellous adventure. This was their job now, being musicians. So there were roaches! Weren't there roaches back in the cramped apartments they'd been able to afford in Boston on what they earned at their stupid time-killing warehouse jobs? There was talk of a cult forming around them.

We are never far from a warehouse in this, the early going. On getting wind of the rift between Goes and Fort Apache, 4AD's ware-house manager, of all people, suggested that the Pixies hook up with Steve Albini, late of Chicago's deafening and discomfiting beatbox-propelled indie antiheroes Big Black and Rapeman. Ivo agreed that the implacably bilious Albini, famous for the naked contempt he har-boured for many of his clients and for working for a straight fee ($1,500 in the Pixies' case) rather than "points" (what percentage would there be in the rubbish the bands who hired him recorded?)

was just the boy to bring out what one reviewer later called the group's "lazy evil".

He did so by acting as though he'd have sooner been nearly anywhere than in Q-Division with a group he would later describe as proffering "blandly entertaining college rock". A record producer's traditional number one job is to make his or her protégés feel confident enough to perform at the peak of their powers, but Albini couldn't be arsed. Aside from insisting that Charles, Joey, and Kim use metal plectrums, Albini seemed to want only to be left alone with his thoughts. He hated recording vocals (and reportedly nearly didn't live through the recording of the "ri ri ri" harmonies on 'River Euphrates'), so of the two weeks they had to record the album, he conceded only two days to vocals. Having earlier gone on record as hating "anything human-sounding," he recorded Charles' voice through a guitar distortion pedal to make 'Something Against You' even more discomfiting than it would have been if left to its own devices. He misogynistically described anything not to his liking as "pussy" ("non-pussy" being the closest thing in his vocabulary to a term of approbation) and made clear that he wanted his credit to read 'Recorded by' rather than 'Produced by'. God forbid anyone should think he'd help in any way to (I can't resist!) mould the "patchwork pinch-loaf" (as he'd later describe it) the Pixies were extruding.

And it worked. Packed, as Nirvana's official biographer would one day declare in a dizzyingly mixed metaphor, with "vivid, violent psychotic cartoons you could hum in the shower", the album – entitled *Surfer Rosa* in the eleventh hour for fear that punters would think *Gigantic*, the original title, referred to the sepia flamenco cover girl's wonderful breasts – shot up to number two in the British indie charts at a speed that left Ivo Watts-Russell, for one, breathless. One British reviewer credited it with nothing less than "revitalising and re-texturing the fabric of rock'n'roll". They were widely perceived as being the salvation of the sorely besieged guitar band format, which many people seem to regard as inherently noble. John Peel and Simon Mayo played them and played them and played them.

Over the years, the Pixies would do four John Peel Sessions, recording mostly new versions of songs on their albums for Peel to broadcast weeks later. One of the producers with whom they worked was Dale Griffin, earlier of glam rock sensations (and David Bowie protégés) Mott The Hoople. He found them very business-like – the wackiest thing he would later remember their doing in the studio was attempting a version of The Shadows' 'Apache' – and was no less smitten with the sound of Kim's voice than poor Joe Harvard – or, for that matter, Steve Albini, who also admitted years later to admiring David Lovering's drumming – had been back in Boston.

"The future," a prominent reviewer hyperventilated, "has arrived." But of course rock reviewers have been making that declaration 35 times a year since Jon Landau's saying the same thing about Bruce Springsteen got him hired as The Boss' manager and producer, and eventually made him a multimillionaire. "They do more than sound like people who went before them – they force the past to sound like them," *NME*'s man exulted, not entirely coherently. "What sets the Pixies apart," Q reckoned, "are their sudden bursts of memorable pure pop melody and an intuitive understanding of song dynamics."

Whatever he may claim to the contrary, no 21-year-old boy writes songs for any reason other than to get laid, be it by bragging about his virility, at one end of the spectrum, or, on the other, pro-claiming his extraordinary sensitivity by either decrying the world's injustice or confessing his inability to endure it. The one thing you don't do, with your DNA bellowing at you to procreate, is compose a bunch of backing tracks for yourself to shriek over about incest and venereal disease – not unless you've been a patsy through your ado-lescence and are trying to come across all bad and dangerous and twisted, most assuredly not one to be trifled with.

Behold the early songs of Charles M.K. Thompson IV, songs full of incest and disfigurement and venereal disease and general extreme unpleasantness, songs full of sudden, extreme dynamic and rhythmic shifts, and agonised caterwauling.

The hilarious 'I've Been Tired', wherein the singer seemingly responds to a prospective do-gooder lover's heartbreaking tales of Southern deprivation with his own tender revelation that he dreads the ravages of venereal disease, flirts with intelligibility. But just try making sense of most of their early stuff – just try! "Better kick my strand cruiser," Charles sings in 'Ed Is Dead', "to the friendlier oh oh oh oh oh oh." Don't we all feel like that at one time or another?

At one time, the music of Pink Floyd was widely celebrated for making the listener feel as though on LSD. The music of the early Pixies, in contrast, makes one feel as though on PCP – woefully disoriented, and rarely pleasantly so, menaced, as in the midst of a very, very bad dream, trapped in a cartoon produced by child-haters, or front-row centre at the lunatic asylum talent show, witnessing a performance of a band put together by poor Syd Barrett, who after taking too much LSD and being banished from Pink Floyd, had tried to launch a solo career. He played a succession of new songs for one prospective producer, who then asked to hear his favourites again, only to learn that poor Syd had made them up on the spot, and forgotten them the moment he stopped singing – if not while.

No one has ever screamed more bloodchillingly than Charles does on *Come On Pilgrim* and *Surfer Rosa* – especially after sounding so Neil Youngishly girlish a heartbeat before. If you understood punk to have made it unfashionable to play in the odd times so beloved of the prog dinosaurs, guess again. You can see why Charles' stuff appealed to David Lovering, the admitted Rush fan – you rarely know for sure from one beat to the next what time signature you're in. Lots of musicians have made their instruments talk. On the Pixies' first recordings, Joey makes his guitar sound, among other things, like a couple of nutters squawking across an alley at one another.

Anarchic harmonising? Only one other pair of singers in the world (X's John Doe and his apparently tone-deaf bride Exene) ever harmonised less euphoniously than Charles and Kim. People have long celebrated how gorgeously matched were the two voices of The Everly Brothers, or those of Lennon & McCartney, or Graham Nash & Alan Clarke. Well, with Charles and Kim, you get the impression that, far from siblings, the two singers weren't even of the same species. They make Mick Jagger and Keith Richard sound in comparison like The Andrews Sisters. The manic propulsiveness of 'Vamos' evokes the famously anarchic coda of The Yardbirds' version of 'I'm A Man', and 'The Holiday Song' is startlingly reminiscent in places of Blue Oyster Cult's 'Don't Fear The Reaper', but you're more likely to be reminded of the most uncomfortable moment of a David Lynch film on the first Pixies recordings than of a Top 40 hit.

You could call it an awful lot of things, the first music the Pixies recorded, but you couldn't call it bland or unoriginal.

As recorded by Steve Albini, Lovering's drums pack rather more wallop than as recorded by poor Gary Smith, whose microphone placement seems to have been very much more conservative (which is to say close). But it's hard, listening to *Surfer Rosa*, to imagine anyone actually believing the story that the drums were all Albini miked.

Charles had earlier gone on record as wanting his band to be bigger than life, and by the time they arrived for their first British tour supporting the Muses eight days into April 1988, he was doing more than his part. Having regularly got baked and then suffered fierce munchies while recording *Surfer Rosa*, he was no longer the slender young thing who'd served Kim *hummus*, but downright rotund, fortune's fair-haired little fatso.

And they weren't exactly reminding anyone of early Queen or somebody in terms of self-presentation, avoiding eye contact with the audience and dressing like Idaho college freshmen. "Believe me," Charles, whose principal sartorial inspiration seemed to be Gregor Fisher's *Naked Video* antihero Rab C. Nesbitt, was overheard to sigh, not entirely convincingly, "if we could come up with a good angle and costumes, we'd do it, but it's all been done before. So we just go up there in our flannel shirts, one of those Indie American Bands That Don't Give a Shit."

Actually, Charles' aloofness on stage worked well for them. He was the last person on earth you could have pictured hollering, "Yo, London. You feeling all right?" Rare indeed is the tubby little fellow who, on realising that he has the ability to make crowds happy with his voice or guitar, doesn't adapt a vengeful who's-laughing-now swagger, a vibe that invites the boys who used to slap him around in the showers after PE to imagine luscious leggy hotties trying to climb over one another into his dressing room after the last encore. But Charles seemed not even to notice that his audience was there – he had a job of singing and playing to do, and he wasn't going to let anything distract him. Which is the next best thing to being the sort of performer who unmistakably craves his audience's adoration (think Bruce Springsteen, or, for that matter, Freddie Mercury, among many, many others) and has the colossal nerve to go up on stage and demand it.

From the first night, at London's Mean Fiddler, audiences were unperturbed, happily singing along with the band, amazing them, and then demanding encore after encore. "You are the son of a motherfucker," in 'Nimrod's Son', proved a very popular audience participation moment. But if they loved helping Charles with that line, the audience may have loved Kim's singing 'Gigantic' even more. Of course, little the Pixies did seemed not to delight the Brits. "It was," marvelled Charles, "like everyone in the audience was going, 'We get it! We totally get this! We totally love this! This is the best thing that ever happened.' "

Everything was coming up roses.

8

(Vicky's Story)
Total Fucking Asshole Bitch
Motherfucker

HER Perf had like insisted I try jogging with her, and had made me feel guilty. She said how was it fair that she go to the Rat with me, but I wouldn't go jogging with her? I told her I'd taken her to the Rat for her own good, because her taste in music sucked so hard. She laughed like delightedly even though I was perfectly serious, and said that she wanted me to jog with her for *my* good.

"Oh, you do not," I said. "You want me to do it because you're like addicted to it, and Brad can't come over to do it with you every night, and you don't feel safe going alone."

That got a big sort of embarrassed laugh out of her, which felt good, but it didn't make her drop the subject. "Of course I feel safer with a companion," she said. "That goes without saying. But it will do you a world of good. It's a simple matter of physiology. The human body requires vigorous exercise."

I gave in. It wasn't that I didn't enjoy physical stuff. Back in the UK, I'd adored field hockey, and been brilliant at it, but when I got to high school and bloodied that guy's nose, the last thing I needed was for people to think of me as even less feminine.

The first couple of nights with Her Perf were like majorly humiliating. It was all I could do to get to the end of the block before I had to stop to catch my breath. I'd stand there with hands on knees like gasping and wheezing while Her Perf bounced in place telling me how good I was doing, being like super-positive and encouraging. I

The artist as a young man. *(LFI)*

New York, New York, early '88. If they could make it there, they could make it anywhere. And they could make it there. *(Steve Double/Retna)*

Backstage February 17, 1988 at Washington DC's 9.30 Club, which, judging from the walls, specialised in indie bands. *(Jay Blakesberg/Retna)*

Joseph A. Santiago manages a credible Matthew Broderick impersonation in this attractive group shot. *(LFI)*

In concert at Giants Stadium in East Rutherford, NJ, 1989. *(LFI)*

At the Werchter Festival in Belgium, July 1989. Charles seems to be enjoying Kim's presence on stage. Or is he grimacing? *(LFI)*

On stage at the City Hall, Sheffield, October 10, 1989. *(Band Photo/uppa.co.uk)*

Charles contemplates his expanding midsection as Joey grows facial hair. *(LFI)*

At the Palace of Fine Arts, a popular site for weddings, San Francisco. *(LFI)*

The tart-tongued Steve Albini, who disliked recording vocals. *(SIN/Corbis)*

Throwing Muses, with whom our heroes enjoyed singalongs. *(Tim Hall/Redferns)*

In Utrecht, September 25, 1990. *(Image supplied courtesy of Kevin Cummins)*

An unapologetically horizontal Charles in Utrecht, September 25, 1990.
(Image Supplied courtesy of Kevin Cummins)

La Deal on stage at Reading Festival, August 26, 1990. *(Andy Soloman/Rex Features)*

The Breeders. Spot the Deal twins and win valuable prizes! *(LFI)*

The artist known then as Black Francis, with the whole world in his hands.
(Steve Double/Retna)

wanted to get my hands around her neck and squeeze with all my might until she like ceased to struggle. "It's hard for everybody at first," she said. "But if you keep trying, I promise you it's going to get much easier. Trust me, Vic."

The good thing was that she didn't insist I keep running – when I couldn't run any farther, I got to walk awhile. By the fourth night, I was making it to Belmont Street without having to walk at all. Then, on the sixth night, when Brad was along and I like desperately didn't want to seem a wuss in front of him, I kept going for like 22 minutes straight. Brad and Her Perf nearly threw like a tickertape parade in my honour, and I had to admit it felt really good for somebody to be so proud of me.

And then I began to like it, and actually look forward to it. The night I found myself disappointed when Her Perf phoned from campus to say she wouldn't be able to jog was the night I knew I was hooked.

The more I liked it, the more weight just like fell off me, and the more weight that fell off me, the more I got smiled at as I walked across campus. Guys in my classes began like striking up conversations with me. One of them, Carl, from my film class, mentioned that he was majorly into music – Throwing Muses being his favourite band – and went to the Rat sometimes. When I told him I went there too, but had never seen the Muses, he said maybe we could see them together some time. It wasn't like asking me out, but it was awfully close, and he didn't even have horrible skin.

It all made me more confident than I'd ever felt, and confidence was exactly what I needed now that the money I'd saved working at Taco Bell my senior year of high school was almost used up. Mr. Basta, my counsellor, had always told me that the happiest people aren't those making the most money, but doing what they love. I didn't see why that shouldn't be just as true for a college sophomore as for somebody out in the real world, so instead of applying for a lot of like demeaning fast food jobs, I decided to try to do something related to what I'd come to love most in the world – music.

I put in applications at Newbury Comics, and Strawberry Records, and the Record Garage, which, according to the *Phoenix*, was where local musicians not only bought their stuff, but also hung out, and at the Cambridge Music Complex. I didn't hear from any of them, and was about to resign myself to having to wear another stupid hideous polyester uniform and a fake grin while taking people's orders for junk food to keep my half of the rent paid when a guy from the CMC called and asked if I could do janitorial work. I figured I'd been doing it on a small scale cleaning up after my dad for years, and the next thing you knew, instead of a demeaning job I hated at a Burger King or McDonald's, I had a demeaning job I absolutely loved where a lot of the coolest bands in town rehearsed.

My boss, Eddie Pollard, had like cryogenically frozen himself in like 1975. His hair was very Ronnie Wood. He wore scarves and bracelets and a lot of rings, and generally looked like he hoped Aerosmith would wander by and like mistake him for one of their own. He probably weighed 120 pounds holding an amplifier top. I'd have bet it had taken teams of wild horses to get him out of his bellbottoms. He reeked of the French cigarettes he never stopped smoking. I thought he might be gay.

He wasn't exactly Mr. Warmth. With other old-fashioned types, he was pretty friendly and like demonstrative, but around the younger, shorter-haired groups he had a way of seeming bored and inconvenienced, no matter what they wanted from him. But he wasn't a dickhead. When he noticed that I was reliable and conscientious, he asked if I could bear to give up ashtray-emptying and work instead at the front desk, taking payments and doing scheduling. I hadn't realised he had a sense of humour. I couldn't have been more thrilled to accept the promotion, and was soon on a nodding-hello basis with some of the biggest names in Boston rock.

I went home to Eastie the Saturday after me and Carl had our first conversation. Tricia was there with her 26-year-old boyfriend Dennis, but my dad was actually out. Every few days, Tricia said, he managed to drag himself over to the bar on the corner to do his drinking. "Well," Tricia insisted, "isn't that like wonderful, that he's getting out of the house?" I was worried that he was doing it just not to be around Dennis, who was fairly scary-looking, with his shaved head and tattooed neck and scalp and missing bottom front tooth. And he wasn't exactly like cordial. He had a surprisingly limp handshake and didn't make eye contact as he grunted, "How you doing?"

when Tricia introduced us. It occurred to me that there probably weren't two people in Massachusetts more like dissimilar than him and Her Perf.

Our pleasantries exchanged (sarcasm!), he told Tricia to make him some coffee. That is, he didn't ask her, but told her. He didn't even say, "Make me some coffee, will you?" which would have sounded a little gentler somehow. He said, "Make me some coffee," like she was his slave or something. And the really bad part is she went over to do it without even thinking.

"I understand you're a chef," I said as we sat down on opposite ends of my dad's majorly ratty sofa, avoiding the exposed springs.

He snorted in like disdain. "That's one way of putting it, I suppose. It's not like those people know what they're eating. I just like open cans, heat what's in them, and plop it on the plates. Hey, you don't got a cigarette, do you?"

"I don't smoke. If you don't enjoy that work, what work would you like to be doing instead?" I was just trying to make small talk until his coffee was ready, just trying to show an interest. But he was like majorly offended.

"What do you want to know for?" he demanded without making eye contact.

"Dennis likes to race motorbikes," Tricia contributed from the kitchen.

"How about," Dennis called to her like disgustedly, "if you just get the coffee made, all right? I can handle this."

I looked at Tricia. There were a lot of things I wanted to say to this asshole about how to treat my stepsister, but the look she gave back said, Please don't start.

Dennis slurped his coffee. I told him it was really nice to meet him. He made eye contact long enough to try to see if I was being sarcastic, but I made a point of looking like ambiguous. He looked away and grunted, "Cool." A major charmer.

Him and Tricia went out and I did the sinkful of dishes. Making coffee was like the most domestic thing I'd ever seen Tricia do. I couldn't go looking for my dad because I was still too young for bars, and didn't have fake ID like Tricia. I answered the phone.

It was Nanci, my runaway stepmum, who hadn't abandoned just

my dad, but her own daughter – Nanci, the bitch of the millennium. She was a few blocks away, in a coffee shop on Sumner. She wanted to see us.

A big part of me wanted to scream at her to fuck herself and then hang up, but I owed it to my dad and Tricia not to. "Do you have any idea," I said, "how much you've hurt everybody? Do you have like any fucking idea?" I could almost hear her like wincing over the phone.

"Come talk to me, Vicky," she said. "Let me explain some things, OK? Do the two years I was a damned good stepmum to you earn 15 minutes of your time, face to face?"

I met her. I hadn't remembered how deep the lines in her forehead and to either side of her mouth were. Her hair was still like the guy's in Mötley Crüe, long and layered and spiky and black as ink. The guy she was with looked like a 45-year-old lorry driver from Southie in a rock star wig, all like beefy and bloated and red-faced, with a noseful of broken capillaries, but with a groovy young heavy metal rock god's spiky hair. And scarves, of the sort the dude in Aerosmith ties to his microphone stand. It was so corny I could have burst out laughing if the sight of her didn't make me want to cry.

She stood up when I came in and obviously wanted to hug me. Fat fucking chance. I wasn't going to cry in front of her – I just wasn't. Her ridiculous boyfriend stood up too. She introduced him. He offered me his hand and said, "Real pleasure to meet you, Victoria." I just snarled at him without taking his stupid hand. "Nobody calls me Victoria." He looked majorly embarrassed, and I felt bad about that, but I was feeling much worse about a lot of other things. I wasn't going to let her see me cry.

We sat down, me across from them. I wasn't going to let her see me cry. I said, "So what have you been up to the past two years?" with like sarcastic nonchalance.

It was her who cried, her whose excessive mascara began to trickle down her face. "Oh, Vic," she said. "Do you really hate me so much? Does Tricia?"

I'd have expected that her tears would make my own flow, but they only made me want to hurt her more. "If anything, I expect Tricia and my dad hate you a lot more than I do. Just what the fuck did you think you were doing disappearing on us like you did? And if you say one fucking syllable about needing to find yourself, I'll make myself sick all over your hideous fucking stupid dyed Mötley Crüe hair."

Well, I'd held out a lot longer than I'd thought I would. Now I absolutely exploded in tears. I felt like I might split open. The table shook. The ashtray clattered on it.

Her boyfriend came around the table and held me. He looked like a bad joke, but he had a heart. I found myself holding onto his arm, this guy I'd known for 54 seconds. Nanci reached over and squeezed my hand. I calmed down. There were no other customers in the place, but the Korean or whatever couple who owned it were like aghast. They looked away quickly.

"I couldn't deal with your dad's drinking," she said. "I tried in every way I could think of, and nothing worked."

"So you left me and Tricia to deal with it. You total fucking asshole bitch motherfucker."

She sighed. She looked down at her hands. She was wearing enough rings to stock a jewellery store. They weren't a young woman's hands, not by any means. "If you think I've gone an hour since I left without feeling like I have a knife in my heart, you're wrong. Total fucking asshole bitch motherfucker's putting it too gently. But I'm going to make it up to her. I am, Vic." She reached into her motorcycle jacket and found an envelope in the breast pocket. She put it on the table between us. "She'll be starting college next year, right? There's $1,820 in this for her college. It's what I've been able to save for her since I split. I don't make as much as I wish I did."

She was a waitress in a Friendly's, and made some extra money as the singer in the covers band that Ridiculous Boyfriend – Derek – was the manager of. They did a lot of Heart, a lot of Pat Benatar, even some Madonna and Cyndi Lauper for more conservative audiences. "I've got another envelope for your dad, for your and Tricia's room and board since I left. It isn't as much – $650 – but this isn't the last of it. I'll be sending Tricia and your dad 60 per cent of what I've earned after I've paid my expenses each month until they think – they, not me – think we're even. We live in a little shithole studio down in Quincy. $495 a month. I don't care if it takes the next 10 years. I'll make it right."

"Like it's about money," I said. "Like there's enough money in the world to make up for how much you hurt everybody. You bitch."

She looked out the window at the horrible bleakness. "Of course there isn't," she said. "Of course there isn't. And I'll carry the guilt of that to my deathbed. But I can't un-leave, Vic. I can't go back in time. I did what I did, and it was unspeakable, but I can't un-do it. I'm trying to do all that's in my power to do. I've wanted for months to see you, and – I'll be honest – especially Tricia. It was so hard working up the courage to finally phone. I'll never abandon her again. I'll be there for her the rest of my life if she'll let me."

I was crying again. "And my dad? He doesn't deserve any like consideration? You didn't hurt him too so bad that he just about didn't live through it? Your leaving wasn't what changed him from an alcoholic who was just about coping into an alcoholic who it's a big deal if he manages to go out to a bar to get drunk instead of just staying in front of the TV?"

I was yelling now. Ridiculous Boyfriend had actually like recoiled, had leaned back to get a little farther from the blast furnace of my anger.

"Miss," the poor little bastard who owned the place, Korean or Vietnamese or who knew what, came over to say, like sheepishly, "must be quieter, please. This nice place. Respectable, not shouty."

"Fuck off!" I screamed at him, getting to my feet, making him recoil, making him assume some like Asian martial arts defensive stance. "What, am I disturbing your other customers or something? Well, this just in: there *are* no other customers! And this place isn't respectable at all. It's a fucking dump."

Ridiculous Boyfriend led me gently outside. I was just beside myself now, sobbing, dizzy, gasping for air, clinging to him like Kate Winslet to a hunk of like flotsam at the end of *Titanic*. Inside, Nanci had her face buried in her hands and was shaking with sobs of her own, and the little Asian couple, judging from the looks on their faces, were trying to remember what had made them leave wherever it was they were originally from.

When I got back to Cambridge around half past six, Tiffani was still at her homeless shelter being a saint. I needed like desperately to run to relax myself, to sweat out all the hurt and confusion and guilt – how could I have been more of a bitch to poor Derek, who'd been nothing but kind and gentle with me? If I had to run alone for the first time, then that was the way it would have to be. I took a new tape I'd bought at Newbury Comics early in the week, a really cool new local group called the Pixies, with a singer who screamed like I wished I could scream that afternoon, that like cathartically.

It felt so good I thought I might never stop. I'd got up to around half an hour a night with Her Perf, but was still going strong, feeling better and better, enjoying my new tape big time, at 45 minutes, and then 50. I was running in place at the corner of Lowell and Somerville when two knuckleheads in a pranged-up yellow muscle car, a Camaro or something, pulled up alongside me and started hooting, which I wouldn't even have heard if Side 2 of my tape hadn't finished just as I got to the corner.

"You call that jiggling?" the passenger dude yelled. In the heavy duty sports bra I bought at Her Perf's recommendation right after she first got me running, I don't jiggle in the slightest. If it had been her and me, we'd have ignored them – if we got into a shouting match or other conversation with every numbskull who hollered at Her Perf when we were out jogging, we'd never have got any jogging done. But my endorphins were making me feel too powerful to let it go.

I took off my headphones, and, still bouncing in place, told the guy, "You want to get in a shouting match, asswipe? Well, let me figure out how to lose 100 IQ points first so it'll be even." There were no cars coming on Lowell, so I ran into the street even though the light hadn't changed. The Camaro pulled right in front of me, and the two knuckleheads jumped out. "What did you say, bitch?" the one on the passenger side demanded. "You want to repeat that for us?"

I went to kick him, but he sidestepped me and managed to snag my leg. I fell hard on my back. They were both glaring down at me. The one in the Patriots cap snatched my headphones off my head and flung them into the street. The one in the Celtics jersey spat on me, on my left shoulder. The one in the Patriots cap saw that I was holding onto my Walkman for dear life, and like wrenched it out of my hands. He took the tape out. "What the fuck is the Pixies?" he demanded. "Sounds like faggot music."

"So you can read!" I pretended to marvel. "Well, colour me surprised."

"They're awesome, dude," the one in the Celtics T-shirt said. "I saw them at the Rat. The singer's a fuckin' mental patient. Screams like a fuckin' pit bull's got his balls in its fuckin' jaws. You got awesome musical taste, girlfriend."

"And you've got a brain the size of a peanut," I said.

"Some bitches," the one in the Patriots cap said, shaking his head, all mock sadness, "just don't have any idea at all when to shut the fuck up, do they?" He like hurled my Walkman at a spot on the ground a few feet from my head. It shattered into a million pieces. One of them bounced off my cheek about a sixteenth of an inch, it felt like, from my eye.

"You ought to do something about your anger issues, bitch," Celtics said. "Next time it might be a pair of dudes hard up enough to rape somebody as ugly as you."

"Hard up is the only hard a dickhead like you ever gets," I like roared back at him, but he was back behind the steering wheel before I could get it all said.

There was no traffic and no like passers-by. I just laid there rubbing my cheek and looking up at the streetlights for like two minutes before I finally got up and dusted myself off. There wasn't enough left of my Walkman even to pick up. But they'd left me my new tape.

When I got home, I burst into tears all over again. It was a wonder my tear glands were still working after what they'd been through since I saw Nanci in Eastie what seemed like weeks ago. I hoped I'd be able to stop before Her Perf got home. I didn't think I'd be able to bear her being all sympathetic and wonderful, not after she'd just spent hours being saintly. It was just a good thing that Walkmans seemed to be getting less expensive all the time.

I finally got cried out again. I took the longest, hottest shower in history. I could certainly understand rape victims feeling dirty. The two knuckleheads hadn't even touched me and I still felt filthy.

The phone rang. It was almost always for Her Perf, some like smitten fellow premed student calling to ask if she'd go out with him, unaware that she and Brad were going steady, as she actually put it. These guys usually lost their nerve after around six rings. We didn't have an answering machine.

It was up around a dozen rings now, and getting on my nerves big time. I picked it up and like snapped, "Tiffani Cohen's residence, but she isn't home now, OK?" expecting that the little terrified premed wuss on the other end would just gasp, "Sure, OK," and hang up. But whoever it was said, "I need to speak to Vicky," in this like really desperate voice.

It was Dennis, Mr. Tattooedhead, Tricia's 26-year-old boyfriend. She'd told him she wasn't going to see him anymore. He couldn't bear it, and I had to do something.

God, how embarrassing, I thought – a 26-year-old getting dumped by a 17-year-old high school girl? How was he going to face the other cooks in the convalescent hospital? And yes, I *was* being awful.

It was my fault, he said, for making Tricia promise that if he ever touched her again she'd leave him. It was my responsibility to get her back for him. He couldn't possibly live without her. He'd do something crazy and desperate if I didn't help – go into a Burger King or something and just start shooting. All those people's blood would be on my hands.

He'd taken her to his favourite bar again to watch him play pool. He drank a lot of beer when he played. It seemed to help his game. When he got back from peeing, she was talking to this dude he didn't know. He didn't break his cue stick over the dude's head – wasn't that proof that he was trying to curb his violent side, just like he'd promised Tricia he would? – but just tried to get her to go outside with him so he could explain how much it . . . hurt his feelings when she talked to other dudes the second he stepped away. It took him quite a while to get out the part about his feelings being hurt. She claimed he'd bruised her shoulder when he grabbed her, but he insisted he hadn't been rough. I just had to help him. He couldn't go on without her.

I liked his having dropped the part about shooting up a Burger King. I told him I'd phone Tricia and see what I could figure out. I made clear I wasn't making any promises – if he really had been rough with her again, there was no way in the world I was going to try to change her mind. I told him he could call me the next afternoon at work if he wanted to. I'd have been lying if I'd said I didn't enjoy having so much power over him.

9

Inconceivable Cool

COULD anyone fault Charles for feeling as though he were living a dream? "To suddenly be in Europe for the first time," he marvelled, "in front of 5,000 Belgian kids, and they're all shouting along with this crazy little ditty you scrawled. It's like, what sort of dream did I step into?!"

The Pixies and Throwing Muses got to be major buds, bellowing along in their tour bus with their favourite cassettes. Somebody wrote that the pair of them constituted the strongest double bill since the Romans put Christians and lions on the same show. On the strength of *Surfer Rosa*'s lofty standing in the chart, the Pixies were invited to headline at some venues. The Muses actually seemed happy for them. How could life have been sweeter?

In the face of British audiences' burgeoning reverence, Charles felt called upon to protest his and his mob's not being so very different from the punters, not really. "We're just ordinary guys and an ordinary gal," he was heard to point out, as you'll never hear an actually ordinary person having to do. "I'm just Mr. Normal, Mr. Square, Mr. Nerd. I like the fact that none of us are rock'n'roll type people. We're truly naïve, so it's pure."

Noting that they closed their shows with 'In Heaven' from David Lynch's *Eraserhead*, journalists began hounding Mr. Normal Square Nerd about the filmmaker's influence on his songwriting. He spoke of Lynch with great enthusiasm for a while, but then seemed to get sick of the question. "I like Lynch's movies a lot," he assured *The Observer*, "but I can't go along with this idea that, like him, I'm a chronicler of the underbelly of America. My songs aren't Polaroids of America. They're just little ditties."

Not that he did a lot of snarling. Indeed, sharp-eyed British press had hardly failed to note the vast disparity between his bland, Charlie Brown-ish appearance and affable manner on the one hand and bloodcurdling screaming and macabre subject matter on the other. "I always liked the image of the moon being freezing cold on one side and blistering hot on the other," he explained pleasantly, wearing a black T-shirt depicting a machine-gun-toting ghoul above the caption "I was killing when killing wasn't cool".

They got home from Europe in May and played the Rat. When Joey turned up at the sound check, he was amazed to see a line around the block. Kim and Tanya Donelly of the Muses (whose name Kim, for reasons of her own, pronounced to rhyme with nooses) decided, probably under the influence of potent intoxicants, that recording a disco smash together would assure their financial futures – this indie rock celebrity was all well and good, but would it buy you a Cadillac? They recorded a demo with Gary Smith at Fort Apache with the Muses' rhythm section, played a gig at the Rat as The Breeders, which Kim and Kelley had called themselves back in Dayton, and went back to real life.

Seemingly a little ambivalent about how ecstatically audiences had been responding to the Kim-sung and co-written 'Gigantic' – which, re-recorded along with 'River Euphrates' by the increasingly fashionable scouser producer Gil Norton, had topped the UK indie chart – Charles didn't manifest gigantic enthusiasm for the songs she offered for inclusion into their repertoire. It was unmistakably Charles' view that the Pixies, if they were smart, would play Charles Thompson songs – and only Charles Thompson songs. Others' songs . . . well, they sucked, didn't they? Their British agent was pleading with them to get back across the pond, this time as undisputed headliners, and here they were getting the unpleasant feeling that, however much they'd enjoyed one another's company in the foetid Kenmore Square rehearsal space, and in David's dad's garage, and in the sardine can that had been the van they'd shared with the Muses, maybe they weren't quite as mad for each other as originally thought.

All of which was pretty easily forgotten, though, in the face of their having become The Beatles, in the face of it becoming commonplace for them to turn up at a venue for a late-afternoon sound check and find 150 kids – who'd squeal excitedly at the mere sight of them – queuing for tickets.

And honestly, what was the problem? Wouldn't anybody agree that the demos Charles and Joey had made for the songs Charles had written for their forthcoming *Whore* album were terrific? Didn't no less than Gil Norton, who'd produced everyone from the extremely hip Echo & The Bunnymen to the extremely unhip Wet Wet Wet, think them nothing less than phenomenal?

Norton, one of whose fondest early memories was of listening to a Merseybeat band rehearse in the warehouse across the road from his parents' home in Liverpool City Centre, had hoped as a young fellow to become a double bassist, but his school hadn't had one, so he'd played trumpet instead. At 19, all bright-eyed and newly A-levelled, he was offered a job making tea at Liverpool's Amazon Studios. He'd never particularly intended to become a producer, but on noting that he could tune not only guitars, but drums as well, the studios' patrons began soliciting his opinion. He was soon producing the Bunnymen.

Having been recommended to Ivo Watts-Russell by his own manager, John Reid, Norton came to Boston to confer with Throwing Muses, and was impressed with the fact that Americans, still into Hüsker Dü and X, were much more about guitars than electronics. As Gary Smith had before him, he saw the Pixies open for a sold-out Sunday night Muses show at the Rat – without Kim, one of whose family was ill – and found them phenomenal. He loved Charles' voice, the band's energy, the whole, well, dynamic.

In years to come, much would be made of the Pixies' remarkable dynamism – entirely too much. Otherwise sensible critics and commentators have suggested that Nirvana, for instance, would have languished in obscurity before giving up rock'n'roll to become lumberjacks or alcoholics or alcoholic lumberjacks if the Pixies hadn't had the brilliant idea of playing softly in the verses and then very, very loudly in the choruses.

'Tis preposterous. Producers had been pulling out all the stops in choruses since the year dot, and the Pixies were hardly the first to realise the awesome power of contrast, or that, if you can't add to Part B, you must subtract from Part A. That is, if you haven't got Duane Eddy, a couple of Mellotrons, and The Mormon Tabernacle Choir to bring in on the choruses, take things out of the verses, like the guitars. Hadn't The Cars (from Boston, no less) muted their strings in the verses of some of their many hits, and then fired all their proverbial guns at once on the choruses less than a decade before? They had indeed, and Joey Santiago had not only noticed, but admitted without a trace of shame to having noticed. More recently, and more germanely (as the safe corporate face of New Wave, The Cars might have been tarred and feathered if they'd dared show their [mostly] pretty faces in Jack's Lounge), hadn't Mission Of Burma, darlings of the early-Eighties Boston underground, used the trick to memorable effect years before Charles and Joey played 'In The Midnight Hour' together?

Charles Michael Kittridge Thompson IV himself would later tell people trying to trick him into saying something wonderfully quotable ("The bastard stole me blind!") about his influence on Kurt Cobain that he didn't really detect that much of an influence, but nobody listened! Otherwise circumspect critics and commentators carried on as though Charles and chums had invented a new chord, one simultaneously as melancholy as a minor but as hopeful as a major, or something. Behold the extraordinary power of Charles' charisma!

We pause to wonder if it would make much less sense to credit the Pixies with having invented the no-bass format later popularised by White Stripes on the night Gil Norton first saw them than with having invented the sound that Kurt Cobain parlayed into remarkable chart success and a life of uninterrupted bliss. But we are only being peevish.

The Pixies and Norton devoted the last six weeks of 1988 to recording the group's second full-length album, first demo-ing it in Juliana Hatfield's dark (illuminated by a single lightbulb!) rehearsal space. Norton, the anti-Albini, made no mystery of the pleasure working with them gave him, delighting particularly in Joey's idiosyncratic playing. "If you asked him to play like another guitarist," he would marvel years later, "he probably wouldn't be able to. But on his own, he was just amazing." On such tracks as 'Here Comes Your Man', Norton meticulously layered multiple guitars in a way that the group had never had the time to even consider doing, seamlessly using a bit of this sound here, and then bits of that sound and the other sound there. He even worked up a string arrangement for 'Monkey Gone To Heaven', in which Charles seemed to be fretting about environmental issues.

The whole band played well, being familiar with the songs from weeks of playing them on stage. If there was one small thing Norton fretted about, it was that many of the songs seemed to be over almost before they'd begun. He got Charles to come over with his acoustic guitar, hoping to persuade him to repeat this bit, to extend that one, but Charles – to whom a three-minute song seemed inconceivably epic – would have none of it. If he'd already sung a particular bit – a chorus, say – why would he want to sing it again?

One afternoon, frustrated with his inability to budge his precocious protégé, Gil suggested they get out for a breath of air. By and by, they found themselves in a record shop. Grinning an I-told-you-so grin, Charles brandished *Buddy Holly's Greatest Hits*, hardly a track of which exceeded 2:15.

Forget what God hath wrought. At the pace of a song per day, the Pixies felt sure they were making something heretofore inconceivably cool on their own, and couldn't stop listening to it, to the point at which poor Gil sometimes had to leave them alone in the control room – but not before pointing out the Rewind and Play buttons on the multi-track so they could listen over and over and over to what they'd made together.

Oh, man, this is *it!*

They called it *Doolittle* in the end, prompting one British critic, trying rather too hard, to observe, "The title suggests that beneath the sound and fury lurks an almost Freudian notion: man as the sick animal, sick precisely because he cannot accept his own animalism."

From the opening bars of the exhilaratingly manic 'Debaser', it was clear that, when they'd chosen Norton as their new producer, the Pixies had chosen well. The sound here is at once beefy and transparent. For once, David Lovering's snare drum sounds like something other than a phone book being struck with the rubber end of a pencil. And subtle, very effective production touches abound, such as the multitracked shouting of the word *chien* on 'Debaser'. On this and such other tracks as 'Wave Of Mutilation', we're clearly hearing a great many (overdubbed) guitars, but their masterful new producer keeps everything in perspective.

If anything, Kim's singing is even more raggedy here than on the Albini and Gary Smith recordings, but behold how chilling the juxtaposition of her little girl voice with Charles' hilarious Peter Lorre imitation is on the second track, on which Charles makes "tame" sound like the most scalding epithet one could hope to shriek at another.

Why Mr. Lovering lets fly a barrage of 16th notes on his snare drum in the coda of 'Here Comes Your Man', only to get fed up and revert to his earlier pattern before the song finishes, is anyone's guess. 'La La Love You', an amusing satire of silly love songs later in the album, demonstrates that Mr. Lovering can carry a tune (if not evoke Al Martino!). One wonders why Norton didn't get him to sing the background part on 'Here Comes Your Man' with Kim, the woeful weediness of whose voice doesn't wear wonderfully.

It seems for a bar or two of 'Mr. Grieves' as though Charles is going to do a Sting impression, but don't get your hopes up, or down. There are echoes of the blues both in his singing and in the guitars here, as on the drum-less 'Silver', but the whole thing's too wilfully disjointed to make much of an impression. Yes, now it can be told: Gil Norton's calming influence notwithstanding, there's still an awful lot of weirdness apparently for its own sake on *Doolittle*.

One can hardly help but enjoy Joey's whammy bar manipulations and little twangfest of a solo on 'There Goes My Gun', even while not enjoying Ms. Deal's determinedly horrid background singing even a little. Joey also shines, through thick mists of reverb, in the midtempo 'Hey', and in 'Dead' as well. The fairly conventionally arranged chorus of 'Gouge Away' confers considerable pleasure. In 'Crackity Jones', apparently inspired by his psychotic roommate in Puerto Rico, Charles actually barks. 'Monkey Gone To Heaven', whose incongruous title line rides on a gorgeous little sliver of melody, makes nice use of cellos.

Word had got around by this time that Charles came up with his songs by standing in front of mirrors and screaming until, with luck, something intelligible popped out. The truth was rather less colourful. "I just write songs like a lot of other people do. I sit around and strum my guitar and try to come up with something interesting. It's not very dramatic. It's like doing homework."

If the good news was that fortune's fair-haired boy was self-effacing, and hadn't come, in the face of the rapturous reviews, to regard himself as God's gift to popular music, the bad news was that, in spite of being ambitious and hard-working in all other ways, he was shamefully careless about his lyrics. "It's just stuff thrown together to fit the rhyme scheme," he'd blithely admit when people began interviewing him, "just words that sound good together. There's so much going on in the world today, so much information bouncing off satellites, that you just have to use the first thing that comes into your head. It's not automatic writing – God spare us – but just sorta brainstorming, very flippant, not like there's any real reference to the topics."

In any great rock song, he would quite correctly assert, the lyrics are the last thing that matter. "I mean, what the hell is 'London Calling'? I don't know anything about stupid English punk politics, but 'London Calling' sounds totally great. That's all it is. Gosh, I'm so tired of people referring to me as hopelessly obscure."

If the shoe fits, pal, wear it.

In the sense that The Cocteau Twins' *Heaven* or *Las Vegas* and the first, eponymous, Innocence Mission album, both utterly unintelligible, are surely two of the best albums of the Nineties, Charles is absolutely right. But is a great chef content to serve newly defrosted peas with his famous poached Atlantic turbot because the turbot is by far the most important part of the meal? Does a great painter not concern herself with the edges of a painting? If a rock record is 98 per cent about beat and melody and atmosphere, that still leaves two per cent. One can either be content to slap a bunch of (sort of) rhymed nonsense atop his melody or try to express intellectually that which the music evokes viscerally. The real greats use that two per cent. The lyrics being the last thing that matters doesn't mean that they don't matter at all.

And of course sometimes a great song can be almost entirely about the words. Consider Paul McCartney's exquisite 'For No One', on The Beatles' *Revolver*. There is no beat, no drums, no bass, no groove. The melody is among the least notable Macca has ever composed. But the words, about the devastation of romantic abandonment! They're nearly every spurned lover's beautifully told story, and deeply, deeply moving.

This isn't for a moment to suggest that all Pixies lyrics lack all power to evoke, but rather that they evoke far, far less than they might have done had Charles been troubled to invest greater sweat and toil.

He told one interviewer that he thought his lyrics akin to Lewis Carroll's famous poem *Jabberwocky*, in that both sounded great and said nothing. Not so. *Jabberwocky*, with its endless made-up words, makes clear from the jump that it's nonsensical, and to be savoured strictly as sound. Charles' early songs do no such thing. When *Gigantic* hears 'Here Comes Your Man', its own favourite, the word *boxcar* jumps out. It inspires visions of plains and grizzled men, hoboes, riding the rails across them. And then, because of Charles' carelessness, we are left high, dry, and frustrated. The family stew? Huh? The nervous walking? Whose? Where? The hanging dirty beard? Huh?

In the end, we'd give back all that "boxcar" has evoked not to be confused by the rest of it. In the end, we would much prefer that Charles had sung it in a language we don't speak.

No wonder the Europeans loved him so much.

10

(Vicky's Story)
Saving Joey Santiago's Hands

I'D got better with my makeup, and discovered that the more I wore, the sluttier I looked, the more attention I got at work from my boss Eddie and his friends. Vicky Tighe, virgin slut. It was pretty clear that Eddie's bud Aiwass, the singer of this embarrassing like heavy metal group called Do What Thou Wilt, was interested in me. What kept me from being flattered was that he was even more old-fashioned than Eddie himself. Eddie might have worn a lot of bracelets, but he hadn't painted his fingernails black, like Aiwass. "Aiwass", I learned (from the man himself, whose real name was Alan) was the spirit who'd supposedly dictated the English Satanist Aleister Crowley's, who'd been like majorly fashionable in the Led Zeppelin/Black Sabbath days, best stuff. Do what thou wilt was apparently his like credo.

I peeked in on a couple of their rehearsals, and it was like stepping into a movie about the early Seventies. The guitarist, Anton, played a mile a minute while whipping himself with his long hair, and the drummer had around a thousand drums, and Aiwass, with his shirt unbuttoned all the way down to the navel, was forever like flinging his own mane of wavy hair around, playing Robert Plant playing the pagan stud. Mötley Crüe had three guys who'd dyed their hair black, and a front man who'd dyed his platinum blond, but if you thought the Wilts (as a lot of the cooler bands called them behind their backs) just imitated them, you were like sorely mistaken – in the Wilts, it was Aiwass who had black hair and the other three platinum blond.

They'd written an album based on Tarot. I thought they were at least three times as funny as Spinal Tap, but they had no sense at all of their own like absurdity. They thought the Boston music scene was completely fucked up, and had plans to do something about it with some of the rituals they'd learned from Crowley.

Many of the bands that rehearsed at CMC were excited about an upcoming show at the Worcester Centre with the Pixies opening up for Throwing Muses. I thought it would be really fun to go. I asked Her Perf if her and Brad wanted to go with me, not because I wanted to be swimming in wholesomeness the whole way there and the whole way home, but because Brad was the only person I knew with a car. Then I remembered that Carl in my film class had blamed his missing an important show, and needing to borrow my notes, on his car breaking down. I took the bull by the horns and asked if he'd like to go with me. I thought it would be like really awkward, and had tried to like steel myself for his saying, "Me go out with you? Be serious!" But by now I was getting smiled at enough on campus to be feeling pretty confident, and he wasn't only like thrilled that I'd asked him, but claimed that he'd been trying to work up the nerve to ask me!

I wasn't the only one who'd heard about the gig. So had Do What Thou Wilt, who weren't nearly as enthusiastic about it as I was. Aiwass and the guitar player, Anton, in fact, were like incensed at the whole idea. "I don't even pretend to understand it, man," Aiwass was saying. "At the very, very least, a band should look cool. The fucking Pixies don't look cool at all."

"They look like four of the dweebiest little fucks at like freshman orientation, is what they look like, dude," Anton agreed. "I mean that singer! Give me a break! Little fuck looks like he ought to be riding past on a bicycle, like tossing newspapers on people's front lawns. And then they've got that little spic guitar player who looks like the houseboy in a fucking Rock Hudson movie, and that chick. Dude! There's a real hottie for you."

Aiwass kept sneaking glances over at me. I think I was supposed to be like amused.

"And that guitar player's just plain weird, dude," Anton mar-velled. "I don't know where he learned to play, but it was the wrong fucking place. I could play better than that with my fucking toes, dude – with my fucking dick."

"And who gets the record deal, man – us or them?"

"They got signed, dude? You're fucking putting me on. No way! By who, dude?"

Aiwass shook his head. "Not one of the majors, man. Thank Satan. By some weird English label. But a deal's a deal. And I hear they're going to be going over there to play next month. Can you get your head around that, man?"

Anton was actually turning red with like indignation. "Dude! The fucking Pixies are going to get to play in England? Oh, that is so, so, so fucked up. England is like Zeppelin's country, Priest's country, Sabbath's country, Def Leppard's, and that fucking paper boy and his band of faggots are going to go play in it instead of us? It boggles the fucking mind, dude."

He adjusted the four rings on his left hand and shook his head again. "Something ought to be done about that, dude. That shit is too unfair to take lying down."

"What do you mean, man?" Aiwass asked.

"I mean, what if the spic houseboy guitar player suddenly found he couldn't play anymore? That would be fucking tragic, wouldn't it, dude?"

I couldn't believe what I was hearing. And the worst part was that I could tell Aiwass thought he was impressing me!

"Absolutely tragic, man. But accidents happen, don't they? And what have we been studying Crowley for if not to help them happen?"

"Right on, dude. I mean, like who knows what Satan has in store for us from one day to the next?"

"Exactly, man," Aiwass agreed. "And if we don't want to bother with the rituals, I know a couple of boys down in Southie who'd gladly do it for a couple of six-packs, man."

"Dirty deeds done dirt cheap, man. Just like in the song."

"They're playing Wednesday night in Worcester, man. Opening for that stupid little girl group. Worcester isn't that far, you know."

I couldn't believe it. He actually thought he was making himself look like really wicked and sexy talking like this in front of me.

I finally got Tricia to return my call. Nanci had called her a couple of times, but Tricia didn't want to see her. I said I thought she should give Nanci a chance. She said we were finished talking about it. She told me what had happened with Dennis. He hadn't really grabbed her roughly enough to bruise her. In fact, he hadn't really grabbed her. Since the black eye incident, he'd been on his best behaviour, really making an effort. She knew it was hard for him because violence was like in like his DNA. He came from a family whose mom had regularly smacked the kids and whose dad had regularly smacked everybody, including the mom. But he'd managed to control it, at least where Tricia was concerned.

The guy he'd got mad at her for talking to, the other pool player? This time, he really had had reason to be jealous. This other guy had been giving Tricia the eye, and she thought he was really cute, lots cuter than Dennis, in fact. So, yes, she'd like brought the whole thing on herself, though she couldn't very well admit that to Dennis. And now she really regretted telling Dennis she wouldn't see him anymore because the cute other guy at the pool bar turned out to be a dick. But she couldn't bring herself to go to Dennis' old folks' home with like hat in hand, because if he told her to fuck off she'd be too humiliated to like go on living. And she couldn't try to patch things up over the phone because he didn't have one.

I gave her an earful about flirting with the other guy right under Dennis' nose, and pointed out that she could have got the guy badly hurt physically. I told her what she'd done had been like majorly immature. "Well, I *am* fucking immature, aren't I?" she said. She rarely said a sentence without fucking in it anymore. "I mean, I'm fucking 17. And since when are you, of all people, a fucking relationships counsellor?"

Me and Dennis met up. He was pleased to come over to Cambridge. He'd probably have come to Pawtucket if I'd asked him. He was a whole different person this time from the one I'd met at my dad's – shy, vulnerable, eager to please. No, desperate to please, to get me on his side. It occurred to me that shyness was probably what had made him seem such a dick at my dad's. With a Red Sox cap on over his tattooed scalp and a turtleneck sweater hiding the tattoos up his neck, he didn't look so intimidating at all. I hadn't realised what pretty grey eyes he had. You could tell he was actually doing his best to maintain some eye contact, though it was hard for him.

I felt like the sun coming out as I told him that Tricia was sorry about what she'd said to him, and hoped they could start over. He began like glowing as I spoke. It was wonderful making somebody feel so much better, and I wondered if I ought to switch to premed myself. (Sarcasm!) He couldn't stop grinning. He couldn't stop thanking me. He wanted to call Tricia right that second. I had to point out that she'd be in class.

There was a long awkward silence. We like realised we were going to have to talk about something other than Tricia, at least for a minute. I asked him what music he liked, expecting him to say like Slayer or something, but he said R.E.M. and U2. He asked why I asked. I said because there was this band I liked that might need my help, and to give it, I'd have to ask his. "Anything, man," he said. "There's nothing you can't ask me."

I asked if he had any friends who were good in a fight. He laughed. Where he was from, a person didn't have any friends who weren't.

We drove to Worcester in Carl's car, his little Subaru, me and him and Dennis and his friend Terry, who not only looked a little like Henry Rollins, but insisted (and he wasn't the sort of guy you argued with) we listen to this live Rollins Band tape he had. After that tape, it didn't matter if Black Francis spent the whole show screaming – the Pixies were still going to sound like The Go-Gos in comparison. 'Burned Beyond Recognition' indeed.

Everybody wanted to know why we had to leave so early. I said I wanted to be there before the Pixies. They wanted to know why. I said I wanted to see them arrive. They teased me about that, especially Carl.

When we got there, though, the guy at the stage door said they were finishing their sound check. I wasn't even sure what a sound check was, which was why I hadn't allowed for their doing one. I asked if we might be able to get in just for the last couple of minutes of it. He wasn't so sure he should let us. I told him we'd driven down all the way from Burlington, and that we were like gigantic fans. I gave him the look I'd seen the little Pat Benatar types at my high school give their football player boyfriends, a look that said I'm so weak and like sexually vulnerable, and if you give me what I want, there's no telling how I'll reward you. Until that moment, I'd always thought I'd feel a complete idiot if I tried that, but it worked. Dudes are so easy when you figure out the way to their G-spots.

The three guy Pixies ignored us, but the girl bass player said, "How you doing?" It didn't look like anybody's hands had been damaged yet. I'd have been like beside myself if Aiwass' and Anton's boys had got to the group before us.

They packed up their guitars and headed out to their van. I told my crew we needed to follow them. "Oh, man," Carl whined, "this is getting like embarrassing now."

"If she says we're following 'em, bro," Dennis told him, "we're following them." It was getting kind of tense, and all the reasons I'd had not to tell anybody what was going on didn't seem very sound anymore. So I spilled it.

"Cool!" Carl said. "Like a rock'n'roll *Mission Impossible* or something. Our mission: save Joey Santiago's hands." I hadn't even known our like beneficiary's name.

We followed the Pixies to a Friendly's, and got a booth near theirs. The girl bass player noticed us and smiled, but the guys were like totally aloof, like they were used to fans following them into coffee shops. I got my crew to eat fast in case the Pixies finished before we did. As it turned out, we sat around drinking coffee for a long time before they were finally ready to go. Carl put his hand on my thigh under the table, not in an aggressive way, but like affectionately. I put my hand on his hand and we gave each other a quick look. I thought my virginity wasn't long for this world. It was an awesome feeling.

When we got back to the auditorium, it occurred to me that our not having backstage passes could be like the fatal flaw in my plan. I found out from Carl what the girl bass player's name was and asked the dude who'd let us in earlier if I could get in to speak to her just a second. He was more like wily this time. "Suppose I said you could," he said. "What would be in it for me?"

I actually felt myself batting my eyelashes. Oh, this was too fucking hilarious! "You're just going to have to take your chances, aren't you?" I said. I couldn't bring myself to skim my tongue along the bottom of my top teeth. I just couldn't do it. But I didn't need to.

I stood in their dressing room door. Once again, the boys were oblivious, but Kim noticed me, and came over to say, "There's no getting rid of you, is there?" Nobody who'd played on a tape I liked had ever spoken to me face to face before. It could have been like utterly nerve-wracking, but she was really down-to-earth and sweet. When I told her I needed four backstage passes, she like guffawed, "Well, somebody's a little greedy tonight, isn't she?" It could hardly have been more embarrassing, but I didn't think I should tell her what was going on, as it might make the group too nervous to play good. And if Aiwass and Anton and their friends didn't show up, I'd look like a psycho. But it all worked out. She got me the passes, these little stick-on things that we put on our sweaters.

We tried to like make ourselves scarce backstage before the show started. There was no sign of Aiwass and Anton. We went out into the actual auditorium just before the group came on stage. They were fantastic. Everything I'd liked about the tape I liked twice as much about the live show. They were deafening. Kim's bass was so loud I could like feel it in my like solar plexus. I'd have given every cent I'd ever earn to be able to play like her. Black Francis' screaming was absolutely bloodcurdling, but you should have seen the smiles on the audience's faces. There was one song where everything stopped for a second and he said, "You are the son of a motherfucker," and everybody like swooned with amusement and delight. And some of it was tuneful too, just like on the tape.

They were doing a song that Black Francis was singing in Spanish, from the sound of it, when I noticed Aiwass and Anton. I immediately stepped away from Dennis and Terry, as I'd warned them I would. I may have wanted to save Joey Santiago's hands, but I also wanted to keep my job.

The pair of big like simian knuckleheads in backwards baseball caps they had with them gave themselves away by being a lot less interested in the band than in the girls in the audience. I couldn't imagine they were going to be much of a problem for Dennis and Terry. As I got nearer, I realised that one of them had been one of the pair who'd hassled me while I was jogging and then smashed my Walkman. I felt just awful about the possibility of his face being rearranged.

Aiwass and Anton, who couldn't have looked more out of place on a bet, were happy to see me. They both gave me a kiss. I was really feeling like a big girl. I think they liked the band's being so loud that they had to put their lips like right in my ear. I didn't think my virginity was long for this world. Aiwass touched the small of my back as he shouted, "Have you ever heard anything that sucked worse than this?" The knucklehead I'd met jogging didn't recognise me with makeup on. I wasn't going to give Aiwass the pleasure of putting my lips in his ear to answer. I just waved goodbye and made my way back to Carl.

We headed backstage after the band's last song, and missed the encore. There were an awful lot of people around, and I couldn't imagine that Aiwass and Anton would try to unleash their knuckleheads with so many witnesses around. It was when the Pixies got outside that I was worried about.

I took Dennis and Terry aside. I wouldn't be able to get them to come to every show the Pixies played, and I wouldn't want to go to every show they played myself. I mean, they were awesome, but I wasn't like obsessive. What needed to happen was for us to send a message to Anton's and Aiwass' goons that they'd regret it big time if they did what they'd been hired to do. "Leave it to me," Dennis said. He looked me right in the eye. I got the feeling he really wanted the chance to impress me, and I gave it to him.

We stayed long enough to watch the Pixies load up their van and drive away in it, none with damaged hands. In Carl's Subaru, Dennis told us how he and Terry had taken the knuckleheads aside. "We told them we'd heard that they might be there to fuck with the Pixies. They denied it, of course. We said it wasn't a fair world . . ."

"Oh, yeah!" Terry like exulted. "That was so cool."

". . . and that even though we didn't think a couple of cool dudes like them would even consider evil shit like that, if we heard of the Pixies having any problems with their hands or feet or fucking toes, for that matter . . ."

"Oh, I loved that part too!" Terry whooped.

". . . me and Terry were going to find them, wherever they lived, and break their faces so bad they'd need their dental records to figure out who they were."

Which was brutal and kind of ugly, but really well written in its own way, I thought.

"You should have seen the looks on their faces," Terry laughed. "They were *that close* to peeing themselves. Hey, how about some Rollins Band?"

Me and Carl dropped off Terry and Dennis and went back to his place to listen to music, but not really. I'd been right about my virginity.

11

On Time and In Tune

SOME months before, in a rare (about as rare as the sun coming up in the morning) moment of flippancy, Charles had told an interviewer he dared imagine his band becoming as popular as U2 without ceasing to be . . . weird. And damned if it didn't seem to be happening! At year's end both *Sounds* and *Melody Maker* named *Surfer Rosa* their Album of the Year. In the readers' polls, it was Pixies, Pixies, Pixies!

"The surrealistic show of sepia splendour that floods [*Doolittle*'s] lyric booklet overflows with a vengeance to seep into the very songs themselves," gushed *NME*'s presumably bouncy Edwin Pouncey, one of those critics unclear on the definition of *literally*. "[The album opens with] a lyric that transforms Dali/Buñuel's film script of *Un Chien Andalou* into a three-minute pop song. Complete with razored eyeball reference, it is an astonishing achievement. Equally thrilling, positively unnerving, is 'Tame', where the rabid pant of a serial killer is superimposed over Kim Deal's breathlessly passionate backing vocal to create a highly potent mix of emotions . . . Who cares if all the words don't appear to fit together properly, or that the picture they eventually show is slightly blurred and chaotic? It all adds to the originality and charm of the band who bring such visions to life . . . The songs on *Doolittle* have the power to make you literally jump out of your skin with excitement . . . From seemingly nowhere the Pixies manage to concoct something that ultimately builds into an epic on a miniature scale."

Q's unnamed reviewer effervesced, "This is clearly the stuff of classic obsessive teen horror nastiness set to a soundtrack of growling guitars." *The Alternative Press*'s Laura DeMarco marvelled, "From the pop tunefulness of 'Here Comes Your Man' and 'There Goes My Gun' to the eerie fatalism of 'Monkey Gone To Heaven' and the noisy anguish of 'Gouge Away', the Pixies . . . express a unique, ardent vision that is both serious and a lot of fun to listen to."

Charles proudly reckoned that, with all sorts of deals now being made on his and the group's behalf – a T-shirt deal here, an overseas publishing deal there – he, at 23, had actually made more than his dad, the publican, the previous year. But he wasn't so big, rich, and important as not to come and help his dad dispense brewskis at Christmas time.

Big enough now to have a roadie (Charles' cousin Mark) who looked after only the guitars, and who, if asked a drum-related question could disdainfully sniff, "Well, why not ask the drum roadie?" the Pixies returned to the UK and Europe for the first leg of a very long international tour entitled *Sex & Death*, opening in Brighton. It was clear that, however flippant they may appear, they took what they were doing very seriously. Before going on stage, they'd hold hands. When they came off it, Charles conducted "inquests" at which everyone was invited to express how he or she thought the show might have been better.

It was no longer just the music papers singing their praises, but mainstream national ones like *The Independent* as well. *Doolittle* entered the UK chart – not the indie one this time, but the one full of artists who owned their own Mediterranean or Caribbean islands – at number eight. A major American label – and a fairly progressive one, that which The Sugarcubes and They Might Be Giants called home – Elektra, signed them. "I'd like to have been around when the Spanish and the Dutch were mapping out the world," Charles pronounced grandly. "It bums me out that there's no land left undiscovered, not even the moon."

In Joey's Manchester hotel room (they may not have reached the separate-limousines-to-gigs stage, but had long since stopped sharing accommodation), Charles strummed an acoustic guitar so fervently as to require medical attention, and was ministered to at hospital by a nurse who identified herself as the girlfriend of one of

The Stone Roses. They went to dinner with Michael Stipe in Holland, and to the pictures with Nick Cave. They hung out with The Cure, whose mastermind, Robert Smith, called them one of his favourite bands, in the cradle of the Renaissance. Charles' younger brother Errol joined them for the swing through the Rhineland. If this wasn't the toppermost of the poppermost, it was unmistakably pretty near.

But in every life, a few drops of rain must fall. Kim crashed her moped in Greece, and, on the way home to Boston, Charles discovered that flying terrified him, as it terrifies any sensible person, and that he felt safe only on Lufthansa.

Not only that, but he was getting misquoted. "No matter what I say into a writer's cassettecorder," he moaned, "the story comes out completely false. I do an interview with a publication, roll into town, read the article the day of the show, and I can't believe what the writer was thinking. Everything is always so inaccurate." In one piece, the writer speculated that Charles' odd stage name had to do with his feelings about his father's alcoholism. "Not only have I never said that," Charles fumed, "but my father *isn't* an alcoholic! The writer opened his story with that. Where did he come up with it?"

A mere 11 days later, they began the 100-show American leg (*F*** or Fight*) tour, mostly opening for The Cure. Hearing about the crash of a United Airlines jet while en route to the airport to catch the plane that would fly him to the first city of the tour, Seattle, Charles used the nearest payphone (these were simpler, mobile-less times) to inform Ken Goes that he would henceforth travel only by bus, car, rail, or luxury ocean liner.

In Los Angeles, the Pixies opened for The Cure at Dodger Stadium, site of the penultimate scheduled Beatles concert in 1966, and didn't much enjoy the experience of playing to scattered groups of fans more interested in comparing one another's new souvenir T-shirts. Not that the club gigs were necessarily better. Charles discovered that he was good and fed up with imbeciles climbing up on his stage to dive back into the audience. And at those gigs where imbeciles were prevented from getting up on stage to dive back into the audience, the security guards were often sadistic brutes, and Charles felt responsible for the harsh treatment his fans received. And the endless hours on the tour bus, the endless hours of Super Mario Bros. and listening to the crew talking about pussy! He couldn't even muster the energy to concentrate on a novel.

And when it wasn't numbingly boring, it could be terrifying, as when, at Burburries in Birmingham, those in the mosh pit got so overexcited that the band frantically waved its road crew over to try to keep their precariously balanced PA speakers from toppling over and crushing someone.

Honestly, Charles had now been all over Europe, and all he could really tell you about the many countries he'd been to was how each had reacted to different Pixies songs. One was reminded of the famous John Lennon answer to a journalist's question about how he'd enjoyed his first visit to Sweden. (To paraphrase: *Dunno. All I've seen is an airport and a limousine and a hotel room and a taxi and a sandwich and an audience and a taxi.*)

Charles had begun to feel, with all the high-powered merchandising by which the group was now surrounded, the programme sales and T-shirt sales and this sales and that sales, like the featured entertainment at a flea market. And it wasn't really working in terms of stimulating record sales. David Lovering, who'd predicted that they'd be big, had had high hopes for *Doolittle*. So it had entered the British chart at number eight. In America, it was . . . a critic's favourite. Big whoop!

All that was the bad news. The good news, at least as far as D. Lovering was concerned, was that the occasional groupie was now being sighted backstage.

Their repertoire became so oppressively overfamiliar that they were able to refer to songs by the first letters in their titles. Trying to keep themselves from dying of boredom, they took, beginning in June 1989, apparently at Zurich's Rote Fabrik, to playing their show in alphabetical order (1. Bone Machine 2. Cactus 3. Caribou 4. Crackity Jones 5. Dead 6. Debaser 7. Gigantic 8. Gouge Away 9. Hey 10. Holiday Song 11. I Bleed 12. Isla de Encanta 13. Levitate Me 14. Mr. Grieves 15. Monkey Gone To Heaven 16. Nimrod's Son 17. No. 13 Baby 18. River Euphrates 19. Tame 20. There Goes My Gun 21. Vamos 22. Wave Of Mutilation 23. Where Is My Mind?), or to starting with the encore, leaving the stage, and waiting for the audience to applaud them back to perform the main part of the show.

The whole notion of encores seemed to be of considerable interest to Charles, at whose suggestion they took to playing an alternative version of 'Wave Of Mutilation', already a part of the show, when their audiences called them back. "It is," he noted proudly, "a *true* encore."

It was puckish, but it wasn't enough, and they began getting on one another's tits. Those lucky fans who managed to get backstage were amazed to find them blanking one another, even after shows at which a sell-out crowd had received them like a new wonder drug that prevented hangovers. Their dressing rooms were now the chilliest place in town. It occurred to Charles that he and the others might not be the bestest, bestest friends ever after all.

The biggest personality gap between the four of them, between Charles and Kim, seemed to be getting wider all the time. For all his maniacal ranting on stage, and his extremely disturbing lyrics, Charles was really Mr. Down-to-Earth, a staunch believer in showing up on time and in tune. For someone who rarely deigned to address his audience, and who'd gone on record as detesting imbecile stage-divers, it turned out he was very mindful of the group's obligation to its audience. Frivolity in all forms seemed to annoy him. He enjoyed getting baked, but wasn't much of a drinker (Gil Norton never saw him have more than one at a time), and not much of a hanger-out. He preferred to stay in with his honey. And he made no bones about wanting The Pixies to be the most . . . professional band extant.

Kim, on the other hand, had been born to party hearty. She was mumsy – the one you could count on to offer you a cup of tea – but no less a good old gal from way back for it, a rock chick with logorrhoea who'd seemingly never met an interview topic she wouldn't discuss as blithely as any other. Her divorce from Mr. John Murphy? *Sure, dude. Whaddaya wanna know?* Masturbation? *Sure, dude. Whaddaya wanna know?* Taking a shit? *Sure, dude.* Her love of Aerosmith, of all people? *Dude!* Sure, she drank too much, but didn't she deserve some credit for not even smoking pot before going on stage?

If you had to pick out a night that exemplified the difference between the two non-Filipino stand-up Pixies, it would almost certainly be that of November 21, 1988. Booked for two shows at the swanky, mirror-lined Citi in actual Boston, the Pixies went on stage at 8.15 on the dot, and played a long set the packed house loved. The moment it finished, Kim, seemingly in need of an adrenaline rush, unstrapped her bass, pushed her way through her adoring public, and leapt in the back of a car containing her former spouse (no implacable grudge-holder, either of the formerly happy couple) and some other friends, and hightailed it over to the Star and Plough, a narrow Cambridge neighbourhood bar in which Joe Harvard's shambolic Country Cousins performed regularly.

Some months before, at the same venue, Kim, with a snootful, had playfully informed Joe that she could sing Hot Chocolate's 'You Sexy Thing' better than he did. He'd given her the chance to prove it, and found the experience as priapically stimulating as *Gigantic* had found the sight of the Ikettes shaking their tail feathers behind Tina Turner the afternoon they performed at the University of California at Los Angeles' Student Union.

Once having finished her debauched gamin version of her song and soaked up the delighted applause of the 50-or-so mismatched student types, local working stiffs, and others who made up the Star and Plough audience, Kim sneaked a peek at her wristwatch and was horrified to realise how little time she had to get back to Citi. She pushed her way through the student types, working stiffs, and others, leapt back in the car, and sped back across the Boston University Bridge, arriving at Citi at exactly the moment she had to strap her bass back on and go back on stage.

That there'd been no trace of her anywhere in the club until the last possible second might not have caused the Pixie boys' blood pressure to increase precipitously. But if it hadn't, why was Joey so overwrought as to try to smash his guitar at set's end (and doing his own sweet hands the greater damage)?

Was it really exhaustion that kept them, after their show in New York the following day, from their own end-of-tour party, or disgust with one another?

12

The Coldest Place in the UK

THE unreliability of Kim's short-term memory might be readily explained, but what about her longer-term memory? At the end of the *Sex And Death* tour, hadn't the disgusted Charles ended the Stuttgart show by kicking an acoustic guitar across the stage at her for turning up late at the gig and then singing out of tune? Maybe the very part of her personality that kept her from rancour toward Mr. John Murphy kept her from realising how annoyed others were with her carelessness.

Which isn't to underestimate the part frustration may have played in the band's burgeoning disharmony. Rather than the chartbuster they'd all hoped for, as noted earlier, *Doolittle* had proved a critic's favourite. Try buying a Ferrari or other rockstarmobile with *that*! Try buying it with David Bowie's having generously described them as the Talking Heads of the Eighties, or with their having dined with Michael Stipe!

Not that their own preciousness wasn't clearly at least partly to blame. People loved the catchy 'Here Comes Your Man', but Charles was embarrassed to play it live, thinking it too confectionery, and the video they deigned to produce on its behalf ridiculed the whole idea of videos. Instead of actually lip-synching, Charles and Kim – inspired by the Talk Talk video for 'It's My Life' in which singer Mark Hollis had an open mouth painted on his face – just held their mouths wide open when they were heard to be singing. Then, to make matters worse, they declined invitations to perform the song on *Arsenio*, for instance. There is no question that they'd have been majorly slimed – it had taken a team of surgeons 36 hours to remove the show's zealously sycophantic host from Jermaine Jackson's rectum after he slithered up it during Michael's most notable brother's appearance – but one either played the game or didn't.

With the tour that had seemed as though it might never end finally over, they got as far from one another as they could. Joey went to the Grand Canyon, David to Jamaica. Charles did the down-to-earth retro thing and bought himself a canary yellow 1986 Cadillac, in which, with his honey at his side, he headed for the coast of his birth. It was his first car since he'd shared an old banger with his brother when they were teenagers.

Halfway across the country, he had reason to thank his lucky stars he'd allowed himself to be talked into making videos. As he drove through El Paso at two in the morning, the Border Patrol noticed his out-of-state (Massachusetts) licence plates, and that he had a CB radio (he'd intended, as Big Caddy Daddy, to commune with truckers, only to cease to be able to stop listening to a They Might Be Giants tape he'd come to adore), and, most damning of all, a broken Mexican *piñata* in his trunk. He'd bought it in Boston as a gift for his nephews, but the Border Patrol saw it as incontestable proof that he'd been south of the border, presumably making a big drug deal. But just as they were about to handcuff him, one of the cops recognised him from MTV. The next thing he knew, they were taking turns posing for Polaroid snapshots with him.

As he'd once sung for his supper at Gary Smith's apartment, he now sang, at hastily arranged solo shows, to furnish his and honey's own new digs in what he called Scumville, better known as Los Angeles. Anyone expecting sensitive acoustic reconsiderations of the Pixies' repertoire at these shows was in for a bumpy ride, as he played a loud electric guitar and shrieked as though the others were there with him.

Kim, for her own part, finally hooked up with Tanya of the Muses, the English bass player Josephine Wiggs, whose band Perfect Disaster had supported the Pixies at their first Mean Fiddler show, and a 19-year-old drummer from Kentucky to rehearse for three weeks and then record together as The Breeders in Edinburgh, in a studio whose roof caved in, with Steve Albini not producing – not for a minute – but merely recording the extremely unadorned-sounding *Pod* album. While the wild guitars of 'Opened', for instance, reminded some of Sonic Youth at their most primal, there was also a bit of melody afoot, and tracks like 'Iris' melded the Pixies' abrasiveness and the Muses' odd tunefulness better than many had expected. The prevailing impression, in spite of its preoccupation with the sordid, was that Kim's stuff was both more benign than Charles' and richly deserving to be heard.

Some months elapsed. Revelling back home in Ohio in *Pod*'s warm reception, Kim waited for Charles to phone from California to tell her when the Pixies would reconvene. But when the phone rang, it wasn't Charles phoning, but 4AD's Debbie Edgeley, who'd got wind of Charles' intention to meet with Joey and David and the group's lawyer to formulate a strategy for drumming Kim out of the corps. Kim should, in Edgeley's view, put her revelling aside and get on the next plane to LA so she could be at the meeting.

How had it come to this – to Charles trying to banish the one person in New England who'd liked his Hüsker Dü/Peter, Paul & Mary ad in the *Phoenix*, the woman he'd plied with *hummus*, the woman with whom he'd sung so happily both in Fort Apache, on stage, and in the van with the Muses? One would like to be able to reveal that she'd had Charles' love child and sold it into white slavery to pay for her addiction to Courvoisier, or something, but nobody outside the band and their lawyer knew the full content of Charles' disgruntlement, and to this day it has remained so.

What is known is that Charles found her chronic tardiness maddening. It is not known, but universally speculated that, in view of *Pod*'s warm reception, he anticipated her demanding a bigger role in Pixie songwriting and singing. She has since claimed that she was in fact quite content just to remain one of Charles' three accompanists, but no less an insider than J.A. Santiago has gone on record as finding this incredible.

In any event, on arriving at the meeting, she was incredulous to discover that both Joey and David were allied with Charles against her. But before they could begin ironing out the terms of her dismissal, it was brought out that, because she was so very popular with the fans (she having assumed the Paul McCartney role of being the only one who actually spoke to them from the stage), the band might have more to lose giving her the old heave-ho than trying one last time to learn to live with her eccentricities. At the point at which 4AD's likely displeasure was noted, Charles began to consider capitulation.

It was beginning to feel very much to him as though the Pixies had passed their sell-by date.

The group returned to the studio, again with Gil Norton, to record their third full-length album, with a budget over three times the size of that they'd had for *Doolittle*. Thinking a bit of variety would be just the ticket, Norton was intent on giving Kim the bigger role she craved, but Charles was at least as intent on no such thing taking place. Trying to get inspired, Charles smoked a great, great deal of cannabis. Failing to get very inspired, at least when it came time for the lyrics, he resorted rather too often to his fallback theme of UFOs. Anyone in doubt that this was the work largely of someone perpetually baked had only to look at the lyrics of 'Ana', the first letters of whose six lines, when read vertically, spelled SURFER.

Twenty years earlier, no one would have failed to exclaim, "Far *out!*"

Discussing *Bossanova*, as they named it, as it was being readied for release, Kim described it as being more Spielberg than David Lynch, more *ET* than *Eraserhead*. A lot of Charles' new tunes, she said, had been . . . pretty, and the band had hesitated to try to make them too abrasive.

Charles did considerably less screaming, but didn't work much harder on his lyrics. Deliberate tempos predominate to a heretofore-unimagined extent. Charles and Kim don't do their famous raggedy harmonising. There can be no contesting that the album's standout track is the gorgeously lyrical 'Havalina', on which Charles' vocal seems buoyed by the very breeze he's singing about. It's a sublime marriage of song, performance, and production. If only – as usual – Charles had taken a bit of care with the lyrics.

The album opens promisingly, with a strangely sinister cover version of an extremely obscure surf instrumental, The Surftones' 'Cecilia Ann'. But 'Rock Music', the following track, featuring some of Charles' most harrowing screaming, makes 'Cecilia Ann' seem in comparison about as threatening as Lawrence Welk's 'Calcutta'. It's intriguing to consider that what we hear here was originally intended as a pilot vocal. (Charles liked his performance so much that he insisted it be retained.) Imagine having to listen to this over and over again while locating different sections of the song!

Oh, but wasn't he full of surprises in those days? The next moment, in 'Velouria', about a girl named after the sort of fabric found on chairs in the homes of persons of deficient taste, he sounds like one of those wistful long-eyelashed crooners in the New Romantic designer bands of the early Eighties. The track features a theremin and isn't very notable otherwise.

By the way, the notion that the Pixies were wonderfully melodic is absurd. As we've noted, slivers of melody are scattered throughout the group's repertoire, as in the vocal lines of 'Here Comes Your Man' and 'Monkey Gone To Heaven', as well as in many of Joey's guitar interludes. But slivers is all they are. Indeed, it is melodically that the likes of 'Velouria' fall down most grievously.

'Ana' opens with a promisingly attractive guitar passage, and features at least one weird-for-its-own-sake chord change. The mid-tempo 'Dig For Fire' features the strangest version of funk guitar ever recorded by native English speakers, but way, way over on the very edge of the stereo landscape, as though Gil wasn't so sure he wanted us to hear it, and yes, only joking. The Descartesian meditation 'All Over The World' features Charles' voice sounding as though recorded through a police megaphone. To suggest even the faintest correspondence between David Byrne's talents and Charles' is to be very silly indeed.

'Stormy Weather' feels like a hook without a song attached – like the last couple of bars of an eight-bar chorus. Another stupid pet trick? 'Is She Weird?' somehow evokes *Alice In Wonderland*, but, as usual, is content with a vague evocation. 'Down To The Well' has strange sound effects in the background, but otherwise makes little impression. 'The Happening' features Charles waxing unusually garrulous while Kim (one hopes) holds a very high note behind him, not very steadily.

4AD released 'Velouria' as a single in advance of the album, in large part to try to get the Pixies on *Top Of The Pops*. But it was

Bananarama, whose own single had entered the chart one place higher, and who, unlike our heroes, hadn't been too cool to shoot a video the programme could broadcast in following weeks, who got the invitation. (The Pixies' shoot-themselves-in-the-foot clip depicts them cavorting in a quarry in extremely slow motion, and makes very clear, as indie bands felt compelled to do in those days, that the last thing in the world they would want is to be played on MTV.)

"The reference point for their sound nowadays," *The Observer* observed, squandering its credibility, "isn't Iggy Pop, but Beach Boy Brian Wilson. Their new songs are harmonically sophisticated, well produced and unabashedly romantic."

"Among these 14 songs," the *NME*, whose test pressing apparently came from a different lot, the non-unabashedly romantic one, observed, "you'll find more references to space travel, aliens, flying saucers and superior civilisations in strange faraway galaxies than in the entire Seventies Bowie back catalogue. *Bossanova* is the Pixies in the Twilight Zone, Black Francis exploring the obscure and the unknown; Carl Sagan with a guitar cranked up to full volume . . . In many ways, *Bossanova* is the composite Pixies LP, the most positive elements of its two predecessors blended together to make one of the most intriguing and listenable albums of the year." The reliably generous *Q* assented: "They give other rockers an object lesson in the first principles of how it should be done. Without in any way mimicking such Sixties artists as the Stones, Hendrix and The Velvet Underground, they combine catchiness (for want of a better word) with a thrilling abrasiveness of sound."

Grumbled about in some quarters for its relative lack of abandon – after 'Rock Music', Charles didn't scream bloodcurdlingly again for the balance of the album – *Bossanova* entered the UK charts at number three in August 1990 in spite of the fact that you never heard it on the radio during the day. Charles professed to be befuddled by his audience's disappointment. "The people," he groused, "who comment on the drastic changes between this record and the last one really aren't listening. Certain things have changed – like having more money to spend on your record, so your 'production values' get a little more sophisticated – but those are obvious. It's as though we were this crazy, wacky, hardcore band before, and now we're a pop band. That's so untrue. To me it's the same old shit." As for his more conservative singing, he explained that he'd been mortified, on hearing tapes of live shows, to realise how much he was screaming. "It sounds," he agonised, "so annoying."

In *The Times*, Barney Hoskyns shuddered, as much as one can be said to shudder in print, at what he observed of the post-modern condition of rock at our heroes' show at the Hammersmith Odeon. "Too sated and jaded to go back to the inane sonic violence of The Stooges, audiences settle for a kind of meta-hardcore, an indie rock music about rock. It is not at all surprising that the Pixies boast a song entitled 'Rock Music'."

Everyone seemed to be doubting one another now. Those in the know wondered if the group weren't being held back by 4AD's reluctance to cut the sort of deals with big retailers that other labels were quite happy to cut. But no one was to worry. If this album didn't do well, there would be another in six months, according to Charles.

Elektra demanded videos. They wanted the band to do 'Dig For Fire', which Charles, ever more uppity, was now heard to condemn as "a bad Talking Heads imitation." He suggested 'Allison' instead. Elektra rolled its corporate eyes and agreed to a compromise – a medley of the two. The wry 'Dig' segment had the Pixies, in motor-cycle leathers, riding in motorcycle sidecars. For 'Allison', Charles, in the same stupid-pet-trick mood that had inspired him to make the first letter of each of the six lines of 'Ana' spell SURFER, suggested they perform the song live (exploiting the miracle of wireless micro-phone technology) on the field of Amsterdam's Olympisch Stadion (that is, stadium). You got the impression they couldn't get far enough away from one another.

After several weeks rehearsing a 90-minute, 32-song set in New Order's facility in Manchester, the last under Gil Norton's tutelage, the band travelled south on the last night of August for its headlining performance at the Reading Festival. Nearly rigid with fear, they opened, after being introduced by John Peel, with 'Cecilia Ann' because Charles was worried that the sight of a million fans (or, depending on whose estimate you believed, 50,000, or 30,000) might paralyse his vocal chords.

It didn't. Oh, boy, but it didn't. The countless thousands sang along joyously as one nearly from the moment Charles himself started singing. He sang his head off — and shrieked, and howled. By the time he unstrapped his guitar and left the stage beaming with those million or 30,000 kids bellowing their adoration at his back, he'd come to feel like Jon Bon Jovi. But by the time he and the others got back to their dressing room, all they seemed able to think about was how little they wanted to be around one another. How many bands would ever experience what they'd just experienced? How many guitar players would quite happily have killed to headline the Reading Festival? And their dressing room was the coldest place in the UK.

If they were ever going to stand together at the ship's prow and bellow, "We're the kings (and queen) of the world!" it was now, but as the always level-headed Charles noted years later, "It wasn't like we were selling millions and millions of records. We were still dealing with corporate people feeling disappointment. They were just thinking about the next big level. Selling a few hundred thousand records is not really a big thing to those people."

13

Kaput

THEY headed once more for Europe, and communed with their fan David Bowie – though they weren't universally thrilled with his Talking-Heads-of-the-Eighties benediction. They went out together in Schuttorf for an Indian, and then, except for Kim (who managed to linger too long in the ladies, and to be left behind), went back to his hotel room for a sneak preview of the forthcoming *Tin Machine* album, none of the songs from which they feverishly shoehorned into their own carefully alphabetised set list.

They played to 6,400 ecstatic Parisiens at the inflatable Le Zenith. They returned to Ireland – where, after their performance at the National Stadium, Bono sent them a laudatory note, which, if they kept it, would almost certainly be worth a small fortune on eBay in 2005. It was a small consolation indeed for their exhaustion and growing disaffection for one another, which Kim seemed to confirm when she informed the audience at London's Brixton Academy that they were witnessing the band's last show.

Charles had it in mind to return to America in grand style this time, and determined, through his agent, that he could earn his and his honey's passage on the QE2 playing three solo shows at London's Borderline. As the ship crossed the Atlantic, he thought of entering the passenger talent contest, but ultimately decided it wouldn't be fair to the aria-singing old ladies who would constitute his competition. Had any of them been counselled to scream like they hate that bitch?

The band had been scheduled to begin a long American tour in

November. *You there, hurry up and feel rejuvenated!* Charles couldn't bear the thought, and called it off, claiming that a close relative had fallen grievously ill, pissing off nearly everyone in the process. *Bossanova* reached number 70 in the American album charts.

And already it was time to record another album. With either Ivo or Ken Goes or both implacably demanding new material, Charles felt as though being made to jump through hoops. And didn't he have the man in the mirror to blame, the one who'd decreed that he alone could write songs for the Pixies? But if they thought he would eat crow and suggest they do some of Kim's stuff, they were sadly mistaken. They wanted a new album? Well, Charles would write them a double album!

A few chords at a time. "He used to come in with more set ideas about the song and stuff," Kim was overheard to marvel, a little censoriously, "like there was always a point to them or something. But with *Bossanova* and this album also, it's been more, y'know, 'Here, this is the song,' and he plays four chords." Even Gil Norton, who seemed half-serious when he joked that 4AD was likely to have him assassinated if he didn't have the album finished in time for the record companies to release it before prospective buyers could exhaust their music budgets on the new Prince and Michael Jackson, was getting annoyed. They'd start work on a lyric-less song – 'Zep (working title)', 'Zep 2 (working title)', or 'Power Ballad (working title)' say – that inspired Gil to see such-and-such a video in his mind's eye. They'd work on it and work on it and work on it (the album would take six months to make, all told), and then discover, when Charles finally coughed up some words, that Gil's video was for another song entirely.

"I had a bunch of music and I hadn't done the vocals yet," Charles would later remember with a shudder, "so I got kind of nervous, 'cause the engineer and the producer were waiting around for me. It was, like, [yelling] 'I can't go to the bathroom, 'cause everyone's looking at me!'"

The four Pixies were seldom glimpsed together in the studio at the same time, inspiring comparisons to the making of The Beatles' *White Album*. Kim confessed to feeling like a guest musician. And the album, finally entitled *Trompe Le Monde*, turned out to contain some of the Pixies' most thrilling stuff, side by side with some of their most dire.

The title track, with the band absolutely blazing away – David Lovering, in his finest hour, seems to have been possessed by the spirit of Keith Moon – behind Charles' breathy, tuneful vocal, gets things off to an exhilarating start. 'Planet Of Sound', in which all Hell breaks loose after Kim's bass dominates for a while, is no less thrilling, with a fab end-of-the-world lead guitar riff that Jimmy Page might be proud to call his own. 'Alec Eiffel', featuring an actual synthesiser at the end to wonderful effect, is similarly fantastically energising. Little wonder that the best Pixies website extant is named in its honour. In the chaotic, scream-laden, virtually unlistenable 'The Sad Punk', it sounds as though the band is doing its best to blow the roof off the studio. Lovering goes wild on his tom-toms while Charles surfs waves of distortion on The Jesus & Mary Chain's 'Head On', which inspires a note that our hero is no hypocrite – in picking a song to cover, he chose one whose lyrics make no more sense than his own.

With the ugly, scream-laden 'U-Mass', which sounds in part rather like the odious Bad Company with migraine headaches, the wheels begin to come off the proverbial cart. 'Palace Of The Brine', whose lyrics suggest that Charles was at the pinnacle of his admiration for the fervently whimsical They Might Be Giants when he wrote it, 'Letter To Memphis', and 'Bird Dream Of The Olympus Mons', which sounds like one of The Psychedelic Furs' less euphonious evocations of the Velvets, should all have been left for a compilation of outtakes. But it's the ugly, tuneless, weird-for-weirdness' sake 'Space (I Believe In)' that represents the album's – and the band's – nadir. "We needed something to . . . fill up the space," Charles sings, before mercilessly belabouring the curious spelling of his guest tabla player's name. We'd never have guessed.

Shameless rubbish. As too is the ugly, idea-less 'Distance Equals Rate Times Time'. Rock Music indeed. Say nothing, either lyrically or musically, but say it abrasively enough and someone's sure to mistake it for . . . art.

'Subbacultcha', sort of a warped 'Theme From *Peter Gunn*', takes a wee step back toward listenability, and features lyrics coherent enough to enable the listener to divine that it's about the singer's finding domestic bliss smuggling drugs with a reformed "erotic vulture". Honestly, Charles, was that so hard? How not to enjoy the sarcasm of "And we listen to the sea and look at the sky in a poetic kind of way/ What you call it when you look at the sky in a poetic kind of way?" And the huge, anthemic, occasionally (in the most important places!) tuneful 'Motorway To Roswell' certainly represents Gil Norton's finest hour as the Pixies' producer. What a great big rousing sound – exactly what we meant a moment ago when we talked about atmosphere!

One wonders, since the word is conspicuously not used in the CD insert copy, if Charles had misgivings about the use of synthesisers. Making a noise with an electronically amplified electric guitar channelled through a battery of effects pedals that could (and do, a million times a night around the world, every night of the year) make the callowest little dweeb's barre chords sound like Zeus in a fury . . . that's pure and noble rock'n'roll. But let the same callow dweeb trigger electronic oscillators via a keyboard, and it's pure vile artifice, a threat to all we hold dear, the anti-rock'n'roll. And what's most galling is that at the end of the day the whole debate, as usual, is really all about coiffures and *machismo*. Synthesisers are contemptible because they're identified with fey electropop bands with annoyingly zany coiffures. Worse, they're horizontal, and just lie there femininely waiting to be played. Electric guitars, on the other hand, are the instrument of choice of virile wildmen with untamed hair – Jimi Hendrix! Ted Nugent! – and unapologetically priapic, and thus inherently marvellous.

Unperturbed by the above rant – and understandably, as it wasn't composed until over a decade later – the Pixies recorded what most listeners agreed was one of the best tracks on a Leonard Cohen tribute album and returned once more to Britain, with Joey's brother Bob playing a supplementary guitar. It was Kim's perception that Charles had liked the idea of unstrapping his own guitar every now and again and stalking the stage à la Nick Cave, though in the end he never actually did it.

They performed for 20,000 at the Crystal Palace Bowl, but 20,000 were 5,000 fewer than the promoters had hoped for. During 'Where

Is My Mind', a punter leapt into and swam across the lake that both separated the band from their audience and rendered the audience's applause at the end of songs nearly inaudible to the band. Like Bogey and Bergman, the group had thought they'd always have Paris, but their show at Le Zenith took ages to sell out.

Back home, Nirvana, whose *Nevermind* was selling more copies in a week than all the Pixies albums combined had sold to date, asked the Pixies to join them on their North American tour. Kurt Cobain, who'd been too shy to permit himself to be introduced to Charles the previous year, "admitted" having ripped off the famous Pixies quiet verse/loud chorus trick, and said that their epochal break-through hit 'Smells Like Teen Spirit' had been his attempt to rewrite 'Debaser'. Charles, to his considerable credit, was having none of it. He quite rightly pointed out yet again that others had been playing quiet verses and loud choruses forever, and said he didn't find 'Teen Spirit' terribly like 'Debaser', as indeed it isn't. The Pixies wound up inviting the Cleveland-bred art-punk (that is, weirdness for its own sake) Pere Ubu, whose keyboardist, Eric Drew Feldman, had played on the new album, to open for them.

Back in the foetid Kenmore Square rehearsal space days, David Lovering had predicted that they'd perform one day at Boston's Orpheum Theater. And now they did, beginning their American tour there. If that gave everyone a lovely warm feeling, and made him remember how much they'd all loved one another back in the days when they left their rehearsals stinking of sewage, they weren't letting on. Charles travelled from gig to gig in his Cadillac, and Kim in a rented car. Only Joey and David were left on the tour bus.

Seeing them in Portland with 3,000 rabid fans, future career civil servant Steve Crawford was struck by their unrelieved (like Hüsker Dü before them, they didn't pause between songs) tinnitus-inducing . . . roar, the like of which he'd never experienced. From the moment they began 'Rock Music' to the last note of 'Head On', he genuinely felt as though his eardrums might explode.

They took a few weeks off, and then, the week before Valentine's Day, performed 'Trompe Le Monde' with the house band of *Late Night With David Letterman*, David Lovering without drums, Kim on a stool. Having not learned their lesson touring stadia with The

Cure, and with Elektra nearly wetting itself in anticipation of the vast numbers of albums it would now be able to sell, they agreed to open for their bud Bono and his band, U2, on the North American leg of their *Zoo TV* tour.

Once again, it was a humbling experience. There was no mention of them on the tickets. Each of U2 got his own dressing room, complete with an Olympic-sized swimming pool, a polo field, and 32 virgins who looked exactly like Cindy Crawford – or at least his own dressing room. The Pixies got one to share, without their name on the door, and found themselves performing mostly to empty seats while U2's fans bought T-shirts and fridge magnets depicting Bono turning water into wine.

Behold the luck of the (Boston) Irish! The tour came to David Lovering's hometown, that with which the Pixies were more closely identified than any other, on St. Patrick's Day. Expecting the local faithful to turn out en masse, the drummer wore his Boston Celtics jersey, and prepared to ride out of the Boston Garden on a tidal wave of adoration.

Guess again, dude. Hardly anyone bothered even to applaud.

Absence wasn't making hearts grow fonder. During a six-week European tour, Charles, who wasn't concealing his eagerness to record a solo album of cover versions with Eric Drew Feldman, didn't exchange a single syllable with Kim, who, with The Breeders, had a new EP about to come out – not *dude*, not *cool*, not *yo*, not even *like*. Elektra didn't seem to be chomping at the bit to get its hands on the Black Francis solo album.

The U2 tour ended in Vancouver, which Charles was known to misperceive as full of lumberjacks, whores, pizza and porno shops, in April. The Pixies played the next night at the Commodore Ballroom. Backstage at the end of the show, Charles, withholding the most inflammatory part of the story, informed the others that he needed a year's sabbatical, and walked out into the night resolved never to do another show as a member of the band with which he had become an international celebrity and Cadillac owner.

The Breeders' released a Kim-produced four-song *Safari* EP, for which they were joined by Ms. Kelley Deal, who'd learned to play a bit of guitar for the occasion. It featured a glorious version of The

Who's subtle Byrds imitation 'So Sad About Us' for which *Gigantic* would have hesitated only briefly to swap all of *Surfer Rosa*. The Breeders accepted Nirvana's invitation to open for them on their European tour.

Charles immersed himself in his covers album, which would turn out not to be a covers album after all. In the course of making a guest appearance, Joey overheard some indiscreet lackey assuring Charles that he hardly needed the Pixies anymore. "When he's in the studio," Charles was overheard to confide, "I get to see the reaction of the other guitar players, who all like him very much, but they're always just blown away by him because they can't believe he does what he does, and how good it sounds. If you see what he's doing, you can say, 'Wow, that's so simple,' or, 'That's so weird. He doesn't have preconceived notions about what he's supposed to do or not supposed to do.' "

On New Year's Eve, Charles faxed Ken Goes a note saying that as far as he was concerned, the Pixies were kaput, and asked that Goes give the others the bad news, which Goes would later claim to have refused to do. Experts noted that Charles' actions were very much in the cowardly tradition of the other Beatles making Brian Epstein sack Pete Best.

Charles went public with his decision in a live-via-satellite interview with BBC Radio 5's *Hit The North* show on January 13, the fateful conversation proceeding as follows:

> *Hit the North: Frank Black* is a solo album, a solo album that you're in full control, but then you were in full control of the Pixies a lot of the time, or so it seemed. You wrote the songs. You sang them. Joey is playing on this record, Kim, we know, is in The Breeders. So you've just fallen out with the drummer of the Pixies then, have you?
>
> *Charles:* "No. I haven't fallen out with anybody, except maybe Black Francis. I sort of have fallen out with him, so therefore out of the Pixies rises something else. I'm just giving it my best shot."
>
> *Hit the North:* Is [sic] the Pixies finished?
>
> *Charles:* "Yeah. In a word, yeah."
>
> *Hit the North:* Why did you need to . . . because it seemed you

had as much control as you needed. Why couldn't you keep the Pixies going because, obviously, it's a name close to a lot of people's hearts?

Charles: "Yeah, some people can pull that off, but a lot of times people just end up boring fans, and stick around a little too long."

If one of the most unmistakable signs of fan boredom is their ceasing to turn up for gigs, and ceasing to buy records, Charles was about, over the course of his solo career, to become very boring indeed.

Charles took poor David Lovering to lunch, ostensibly so he could explain why he'd pulled the plug, but neither had the stomach for the subject, and neither raised it. Joe was similarly inclined just to let the whole thing go. It wasn't that Charles was a jerk – far from it, in fact. It was more that, over the course of their three-quarters of a decade together, the other Pixies had grown used to Charles playing his cards very close to his chest. And why should he be any different now that it was all over?

14

Chewing the Fat

WHAT'S the first thing you do if you've just gone solo, and want to make it as hard as possible for yourself to cash in on the reputation of the very successful band you've just broken up with a fax and a radio interview? If you're Charles Michael Kittridge Thompson IV, and seemingly have a compulsion for shooting yourself in the foot, you start calling yourself by a name your fans don't know. You mothball Black Francis, that is, and adapt Frank Black, a name better suited to the square-jawed fellow who supervises a crew of Latinos who remove asbestos from people's attics, belongs to two bowling leagues, and every night after work has a shot and a beer chaser.

He unveiled his new identity on the same radio programme on which he confirmed the death of the Pixies, telling BBC Radio 5's Mark Radcliffe, "I did it to simplify things. You know, people never really got the old name, or were twisting it around, mixing it up with my real name. So I wanted something a bit more basic, a little more straight ahead, something with a little more oomph."

While recording *Frank Black* (and, for that matter, its follow-up, *Teenager Of The Year*), Charles was frequently asked by the studio receptionist if he wanted to talk to someone phoning to ask about the next Pixies album or tour. Oh, did he. "Forget about the Pixies," he implored his fans through the press. "You bought the records. Play them when you're feeling nostalgic." Later, on tour, he angrily mocked people who called out for Pixies hits.

Which, unless it was 'Gigantic', for which Kim had written the lyrics, made no sense at all. It wasn't like Beatles fans calling out for

'Yesterday' or 'Hey Jude' at John Lennon shows. They were all Charles' bloody songs! Or did he somehow imagine that what everyone liked best about them were Kim's funkless, childish bass lines? How very peevish, our hero!

And how very self-defeating. What's the second thing you do if you've just gone solo, and want to make it as hard as possible for yourself to cash in on the reputation of the very successful band you've just broken up with a fax and a radio interview? Refuse to perform the very songs (although you wrote them yourself, and sang them!) that made the group very successful.

People may imagine that all rock stars do is turn up with starlets on their arms at exhibitions by their favourite artists, get ushered immediately to the best tables of restaurants at which you or I would have to book tables months in advance, and even then have to spend 45 minutes cooling our heels in the bar, or ride around in limousines taking cocaine, but it's actually very much more arduous than that for one who's recently abandoned the group with which he came to fame.

Charles spent most of the first couple of months of his solo career trudging around from radio station to radio station bantering with bozos with mullets, answering the same questions (*Are the Pixies broken up? What's with this wacky new name? Did you happen to bring along a little something for my nose?*) over and over and over and over and over and over and over and over, occasionally getting to perform live on the air with his acoustic guitar, never, so far as is known, bringing in his Telecaster and an amplifier, though they're what he'd used in his earlier solo shows.

A few days before St. Patrick's Day, 1993, he played some of his favourite records on San Diego's alternative station 91X, including Iggy's inevitable 'The Passenger', The Psychedelic Furs' 'Into You Like A Train', whose title he would soon quote in one of his own songs, The Buzzcocks' 'I Believe', The Beatles' under-appreciated 'Savoy Truffle', and The Clash's 'Guns Of Brixton'. Some weeks later, in San Francisco, he was joined in the studio by Eric Drew Feldman, whom the DJ graciously didn't ignore, and who played bass when Charles performed 'Old Black Dawning', 'Czar', and, best of all, 'I Heard Ramona Sing'.

In Providence, WBRU listeners got to hear him do a partial version of The Ramones' 'Beat On The Brat'. Everyone seemed so delighted that he reprised it three days later on MTV. He also appeared on Santa Monica's KCRW, Seattle's KNDD, and San Francisco's Live 105.

Online, *Nude As The News* rather over-generously called Charles' solo album "the expression of an artist fully released from his shackles and turned loose to create a masterpiece . . . Black covers every base that an ex-Pixie fan could truly expect him to and adds more into the mix as well. The songs sound less strained to fit a particular sound or mood, but free to evolve in the fertile imagination of Frank Black. A brilliant debut."

Nonsense.

On record as having little use for the wacky, kitsch approach of The B-52s, Frank here launches his post-Pixies career with a wacky, kitsch meditation on the fact that *Los Angeles* used to be pronounced in films with a hard g. "I met a man," he croons waveringly. "He was a good man." One is reminded of the wonderfully pompous opening lines of Nick Lowe's '(What's So Funny 'Bout) Peace, Love And Understanding'. But aside from nice synth strings and a brief guest appearance by George Harrison (or someone trying to sound like him) on guitar, the track isn't gigantically notable. The mostly acoustic second track, 'I Heard Ramona Sing', is virtually tuneless except for the very engaging title line, and pleasingly much more conventional-sounding than Charles' earlier work, as too is the wacky, kitschy 'Fu Manchu', which features saxophones and synths.

By the time we reach 'Places Named After Numbers', which benefits from yet another propulsive groove, we're thinking that this might be the start of something wonderful. Why, his reworking of Brian Wilson's 'Hang On To Your Ego', could be played in actual discotheques – the kind in which men in tight-fitting shirts with extremely pointed collars try to persuade women with big hair and ankle bracelets to have sex with them – without there being a stampede for the exits! Charles doesn't scream even a little, and the backing track insistently implores, "Dance to me! You know you want to." Later, there's a reasonably enjoyable homage to Iggy, 'Ten

Percenter', in which Charles indulges in some vocal silliness unheard since the Gary Smith recordings.

Elsewhere, though, moments of pleasure are scant indeed. We're probably meant to find his horrible off-key singing in the distortion-clogged 'Czar' exhilaratingly anarchic or something, but *Gigantic* finds it only grating. The scandalously over-arranged 'Every Time I Go Around Here' finds him singing at the very bottom of his range, and consequently sounding strangely Dylan-ish, which in this instance is no compliment. 'Parry The Wind High, Low' features huge dynamic shifts, a theremin, and the rhythm section charging into half-time at the end under endless annoying repetitions of the title line, all to very little effect.

We pause to contemplate the absurdity of this being considered a solo album. Beside Eric Drew on bass, keyboards, and what are here identified as synthetics (*synthesiser* still being a dirty word?) and Nick Vincent (and Bob Giusti) on drums, guitarists Joseph A. Santiago, Moris Tepper (another Valley boy turned Beefheart alumnus), and David Sardy, and saxophonists John Linnell (ordinarily the nasal lead voice of They Might Be Giants and Kurt Hoffman) all pitch in.

Though Ivo would later assert that he'd been pleased, it was Charles' impression that the 4AD kingpin didn't take his solo album very seriously. One could hardly have blamed him. He'd scuttled the Pixies for . . . this?

Those in the know had speculated, in the days before the fateful fax and radio interview that ended the Pixies, that one of Charles' principal gripes was that Kim and David Lovering were something less than the greatest rhythm section in the history of popular music. There can be no denying either that E. D. Feldman, formerly of Captain Beefheart's Magic Band and Pere Ubu, and a product of roughly the same neck of the suburban San Fernando Valley woods that Charles now called home, represented a huge improvement on Kim, or that Nick Vincent (formerly Donny & Marie's stick-and-pedal man [it was a living, one supposes]) is a wonderful drummer. But he scuttled the Pixies for some small improvement in the drumming and considerable improvement in the bass playing?

Oh, these wacky, unpredictable geniuses.

Even the once-proud team of designer Vaughn Oliver (here

joined by Chris Bigg) and photographer Simon Larbalestier drop the ball here – for the second time in a row, *Trompe Le Monde* too having been far, far below the standard they set for themselves on *Come On Pilgrim* and *Surfer Rosa*. One of Larbalestier's photos – of the prodigiously double-chinned Charles looking every inch a Wisconsin dairy farmer – is gloriously funny, but Vaughn superimposes the lyrics of 'Don't Ya Rile 'Em' over it, the song's title in a typeface better suited to the sides of British public housing erected in the early Sixties.

"Just a few years later," *All Music Guide*'s Heather Phares would write a few years later, "new wave-inspired punk-pop bands like Weezer, The Rentals, and even No Doubt ruled alternative rock, proving that even if his solo career wasn't as influential as his Pixies years, Frank Black was still ahead of his time."

In any event, having chewed the fat with more DJs than any American should ever be compelled to, he began his first tour without the Pixies on May 27 in Eugene, Oregon, the birthplace of grunge. The steadfast Joey was there to play lead guitar (now, notably, as a hired hand), along with Eric on keyboards, bassist Tony Maimone, late of Pere Ubu, and Nick Vincent on drums. They informally called themselves the Frank Black Experience, though it hadn't quite the panache of Nine Inch Worm Makes Own Food, to which the future Butthole Surfers had beaten them anyway. *Frankie Goes to Eugene, Portland, Seattle, Vancouver, Chicago, Philadelphia, Cleveland, Toronto, Montreal, Northampton, Boston, Asbury Park, Back to Boston, New York, Mansfield, Massachusetts, Birmingham, Atlanta, Jackson, New Orleans, Houston, Dallas, Los Angeles, Ventura, Back to Los Angeles, and San Francisco* might have had greater panache, but almost surely would have inspired seething resentment in the poor sods who had to put it, letter by letter, on venue marquees.

Whatever you called them, you couldn't call them a band that performed any material associated with the Pixies. Indeed, as noted earlier, anyone impolitic enough to call out for a Pixies song in those days was likely to be ridiculed from the stage by the former lead Pixie. Instead, they did most of the *Frank Black* album, as well as the instrumentals 'Fear (Theme from *One Step Beyond*)' and 'War Of The Satellites', Gene Chandler's 'Duke Of Earl', and, most surprisingly, The Kinks' ode to complacency, 'This Is Where I Belong'. Rarely one to banter with a large audience, Charles between songs commonly mentioned his delight with the Rev. Horton Heat, who opened most of the shows on the tour, a gracious move on his part.

On June 24, the band travelled down to New York City for a live radio broadcast from Electric Ladyland. Halfway through, Charles shocked the nation by inviting his friends They Might Be Giants to come out and warble a couple of their best-loved melodies. But he had no monopoly on lapsed Pixie magnanimity. Joe and his brothers Bob and Lou (*bobaloo!*) were meanwhile playing on a new album by Steve Westfield, whose Pajama Slave Dancers had earlier encouraged such U-Mass bands as Buffalo Tom, Dinosaur – and the Pixies. Joe had in fact produced the Dancers' last album.

Meanwhile, the second Breeders album, *Last Splash*, which Kim had written nearly all of as well as produced, was coming for the multiply pierced and backward-baseball-capped to define that summer. "Like her old band the Pixies without their abrasiveness," marvelled Douglas Wolk, "tomboyish rather than *macho*." It was both the first and last time the word *macho* had ever been or ever would be used to describe the sound of the Pixies. The album's first single 'Cannonball', an expression of La Deal's distaste for the elitism of the Marquis de Sade, seemed to come along at precisely the right moment, one at which pop radio was ready to give exactly such a record a great, great deal of play. It would reach number two in the Modern Rock Tracks charts, propelling the album up to number 34 and, eventually, platinum certification. But if The Breeders' having suddenly become the toast of indie rock made Charles want to tear out handfuls of his own hair, he kept it hidden.

15

The Plummet

AFTER the first Frank Black tour finally finished in San Francisco's Warfield Theater, Charles spent four months recuperating (he was 28 now, and rather less the embodiment of rude animal health he'd been at 22), writing songs, and imagining (mistakenly, according to staff who joined up at around that time) that, while other companies dispensed with suits and high heels (and that's not even mentioning the women, ta-da-*dum*), 4AD marked Friday afternoons by putting on black armbands, turning off all the lights, listening morosely to Pixies albums, and gnashing their teeth.

Then, just after Thanksgiving, presumably still full of turkey, stuffing, pumpkin pie, and other traditional dishes, Charles tried out some of his new songs at four shows at McCabe's Guitar Shop in Santa Monica, to which he would return often in the years to come.

Teenager Of The Year, his second solo album, is best left shrink-wrapped, as it's all downhill after you've been amused by the photo of our unrepentantly rotund hero smirking like a beauty queen on the cover, with a fistful of roses and a tiara doing little to conceal that fortune's fair-haired boy was now losing his fair hair at an alarming clip. There are a couple of nice "synthetics" on a couple of tracks – 'The Vanishing Spies' and 'Speedy Marie', for instance – and an appealingly loony solo by the newly recruited guitar hero Lyle Workman on 'Bad Wicked World'. 'Fiddle Riddle' imagines reggae as having a tack piano instead of a chicken-scratch guitar. The lyrics to 'Abstract Plain', wherein Charles, whining Neil Young-ishly, pines to live on one, are very wry. For the most part, though, it's badly written and composed (*Gigantic* couldn't remember a single melodic phrase by the end of the 22nd song), badly sung, and inattentively produced – 'Sir Rockaby', which has some of the pastoral gentleness of *Nashville Skyline*-period Dylan, cries out plaintively for background vocals, but gets none. Lazy bastards. There's the usual sprinkling of the lyrics with unusual, intriguing words, "thalossacracy", that make promises the songs invariably fail to keep. There's an awful lot of weirdness for its own sake.

One is reminded of the famous joke about the disgruntled old Jewish ladies on holiday in the Catskill Mountains. When one says, "Oy, the food is terrible here," her friend replies, "And such skimpy portions!" Nothing of the sort can happen here, where, in response to the first lady grousing, "Oy, such rotten songs," her friend would reply, "But 22 of them!"

But don't believe me. Believe the fact that, after *Teenager*, 4AD's Ivo reckoned that the label would probably be just as well off without Charles' next solo album. But it was no skin off Charles' nose, because here came Marc Geiger, co-inventor of Lollapalooza, with an offer to join Jesus & Mary Chain, Love & Rockets, Skinny Puppy, and Julian Cope on Rick Rubin's American Recordings roster.

Right after the release of *Frank Black*, word had spread like wildfire that Charles would be included on a forthcoming Otis Blackwell tribute album. Lyle Workman had been one of those who'd heard it, via a mutual guitar builder friend. Having played earlier in the Todd Rundgren-produced Sacramento band Bourgeois Tagg, Lyle attended Charles' session, and at its end advised Charles that he was an avid fan and a musician of appreciable pedigree in his own right, prompting Charles to wonder, "What are you doing next month?"

"Playing with you," Lyle dared to reply. Once out of Charles' sight, he hurriedly placed a call to a friend in Los Angeles to ask if he could sleep on his couch. The friend said sure. Lyle moved down and began phoning Charles' home in the pleasant, bland San Fernando suburb of West Hills to remind him of his determination to be his lead guitarist.

And it worked. Beginning with *Teenager Of The Year*, Lyle was Charles' guitarist for five years – and loved pretty nearly every minute of them. "Charles is the most generous musician I've ever worked with," he would later assure Charles' biographer. "I've never had comparable freedom or space with anyone else I've played for. I didn't actually co-write the songs, but I might as well have, as I was a 100 per cent participant in the music. No matter how wacky or crazy the sound I wanted to make, Charles never said no. It was the best gig I ever had."

Charles wasn't only a generous musical collaborator, Lyle relates with palpable fondness, but a generous man, one who rarely let anyone pay for his own dinner. "And he gave me guitars." In five years, the two never exchanged an angry syllable, though even the most easy-going and mutually affectionate musicians are pretty well guaranteed to be sick of the sight of one another by the end of long tours of the sort on which Charles regularly embarked.

Once having recorded *Teenager Of The Year*, Charles spent the early spring with his band on one such tour, opening for The Ramones, sometimes playing as few as five songs, often playing as many as 15, including several from the second album. They played San Francisco's Warfield and Hollywood's Palladium, Roseland and The Academy in New York City. After bidding the gabba-gabba-hey boys goodbye, they did a couple of shows at the once-prestigious Roxy on Sunset Blvd., and a couple of college gigs. Then, after a three week break, Charles returned to the UK for the first time since the break-up of the Pixies to record a John Peel Session. Unable to afford to bring drummer Nick Vincent and the others over with him, he had to count not on the kindness of strangers, but on that of the sublime Scottish pop band Teenage Fanclub to back him up. He did some TV and radio, enjoyed a doner kebab or two, presumably, and conspired to re-unite with his own band in a few weeks' time in Paris, which, judging from advance sales of tickets to his series of seven shows at the Arapaho Club, couldn't wait to see him again. At the fourth of those Paris shows, he delighted his audience by performing a set alone with his guitar. He did in-store appearances at the Louvre and Champs Elysées Virgin stores, and basked in the strange glow of Gallic approbation, keeping his feelings about being regarded as a genius in a country that venerated Jerry Lewis to himself.

Kim and her infernal Breeders, in the meantime, were finishing a year's touring with a series of rapturously received main-stage performances at 1994's Lollapalooza.

It turned out that Joe and his wife Linda Mallari, whose offer of background singing he'd declined all those years ago, had a group of their own now – The Martinis – Linda, who'd gone on from Emerson College to sing in Holiday Inn cocktail lounges, having learned the requisite few barre chords mere months before their first reportedly deafening show. David Lovering, of all people, did the drumming. They contributed a gorgeous track to the soundtrack of the direct-to-whatever's-one-step-below-video feature film *Empire Records*. But just as they were about to transform their burgeoning following, favourable reviews, and the fawning of record company talent scouts into megabucks, they broke up. For the next couple of years, Joe and Linda went through a great many bass players and drummers, until they finally released an eclectic nine-track demo CD at the start of 1998.

Without much hesitation, *Gigantic* would gladly swap any six Frank Black albums for 'So Free', the *Empire Records* track, a rhythmically insistent, hook-laden little jewel that sounds like the work of the glorious Mazzy Star on antidepressants that are working, as opposed to just killing their libidos. Mrs. Santiago turns out to have an inexpressibly charming falsetto, and uses it to great advantage here. The repeating instrumental motif could hardly be simpler, but sometimes simple's sublime, and this is one of those times.

Back in the USA, Charles and the band appeared on MTV, and on *Late Night With Conan O'Brien*, a former writer for *The Simpsons* gone bad. Conan's straight man sidekick Andy Richter could be glimpsed dancing with frenzied abandon as the band played 'Freedom Rock'. Behold the humiliations to which a straight man sidekick is subjected!

Teenager Of The Year inspired one of the many websites that worship him to rhapsodise, "Frank Black has produced his magnum opus with *Teenager Of The Year* . . . The perfect expression of a pop genius."

Honestly. If you use genius to describe Charles bloody Thompson, what word is left to describe Smokey Robinson, Marvin Gaye,

Stevie Wonder, Elvis Costello, Richard Thompson, and Ron Sexsmith?

Call him what you will, Charles got himself a protégé. Jonny Polonsky, a reformed paratrooper and unashamed Monkees fan and Sixties nostalgist from the Illinois outback, had earlier sent a demo tape to guitarist Reeves Gabrels, former David Bowie collaborator and old family friend, who'd passed it along to Charles, who was much taken with it. They became friendly over the phone, and discovered that they not only admired one another's music, but also shared an interest in weightlifting, sparring, and kickboxing. "We're pretty physical guys," Polonsky would note, though it was a bit hard to believe it of the corpulent Charles. "So we bonded that way . . . as men."

Charles helped his protégé to get a management deal, and then brought him out to California to produce the demo that got him a deal with his own new label, American Recordings, and finally hired Jonny and his band Honky Balls to open for him on the tour to promote his third solo album, *The Cult Of Ray*.

Charles remained unable, after three years' coaxing, to get another might-have-been production protégé – Joseph A. Santiago – to come into the studio with him. It wasn't that he ever actually said no, but rather that he could never bring himself to say yes.

In late August, Frank began a world tour whose first stops included several European festivals – Dublin's Dalymount Sunstroke, Belgium's Hasselt, and Denmark's Heyday, as well as Reading, the Pixies' performance at which not so very long before had left Charles feeling like Jon Bon Jovi. They proceeded to Japan, and to Australia, where they played at Adelaide's memorably named Synagogue Club. Only a week after their performance at Brisbane's Livid Festival, Charles was back in New Haven, opening without the band, as he would continue to do through to New Year's Eve, for They Might Be Giants.

Career civil servant Steve Crawford, whose eardrums had somehow survived the Pixies in Portland a few years before, saw the show. Noticing how little attention the Giants fans paid to Frank, it occurred to him that the only faster plummet from grace he'd ever witnessed in the pop world was that of Vanilla Ice. But if Charles felt dizzy from having gone so quickly from headlining the Reading Festival to being a quirky (if fab) cult band's opening act, he didn't let on. If being someone else's warm-up act at the Orpheum Theater in Boston, of whose stage the young Pixies had once dreamed, felt weird and painful, he still did it with a smile.

Maybe it helped that, once in New York, he was invited to be a guest on the Halloween edition of the Jon Stewart show on Comedy Central. The fly in the ointment being that the great man's producers didn't want Frank Black alone, but with a band. He considered asking the Giants, only to discover that his old pal Conan O'Brien had booked them. Finally, he was able to persuade Scott Boutier and David McCaffrey, the drummer and bass player of the Connecticut R.E.M. soundalikes Miracle Legion, to appear with him. They performed all of 'Headache', and then some of his peppy new opus 'Jumping Bean' under the end credits. Thereafter, Frank would recount, "I got a lot of calls from friends wondering who my new band was. I just took that as a sign that I should play with these guys."

From the start, it had seemed likely that Charles and the Giants would perform together, and Charles did occasionally join them on stage for 'Spy', but it took a while for them to collaborate on a larger scale – and required the intervention of an inattentive agent. Believing their tour would end in Dallas on the evening of December 18, John Linnell had made reservations for a deluxe pre-holiday week abroad, only to learn, too late to change his plans, that the Club 616 had been led to believe it could expect a performance on the evening of December 20. Charles graciously flew back down from Rhode Island, where he'd already begun rehearsing for his forthcoming European band tour, to perform with the Giants remaining – John, Flansburgh, and two of their band, as They Might Be Frank. Their repertoire included Charles' 'Los Angeles', 'Headache', 'Czar', and Charles' peppy new opus 'Jumping Bean', and Giants favourites 'Spy', 'Dig My Grave', 'The Sun', 'Istanbul', and a re-imagined 'Particle Man', with a Bo Diddley beat and Charles playing the clarinet line on the guitar.

In November, Kelley Deal was arrested for possessing heroin. She later admitted to having started shooting up as a teenager, and then being a practising alcoholic in her computer analyst days, her top-secret clearance notwithstanding, and to being surprised by no one seeming to notice that, after staying up all night on ecstasy, she'd commonly show up for work in the same clothes she'd worn the day before. She would spend the first half of the following year in a Minnesota rehab facility. While waiting for her, and the apparently terminally fed up Josephine Wiggs, Kim and Breeders drummer Jim Macpherson formed a just-something-to-keep-busy-with band called Tammy & The Amps, later shortened to The Amps, with a couple of stalwarts from Dayton. They recorded a lo-fi album (Kim having the same irrational dread of digital recording that Charles had come to have of multi-tracking in general) full of loopy stoned-sounded singing, *Pacer*, together and toured the Western democracies with the Foo Fighters and Sonic Youth.

It was a living.

16

The Impulse Was Noble

IN 1996, Frank and the band must have forgotten what their respective homes looked like, as they performed no fewer than 139 shows, both in their own country and in several European countries as well. Most of the American shows were in the biggest clubs in town (although one LA performance was at the Troubadour, which back in their heyday might have been adjudged too small for the Pixies' tune-up room), but they were clubs. Still, there were festivals aplenty – Sweden's Hultsfred, the Czech Republic's Jam '96, Germany's Rockpalastl, Denmark's Roskilde, France's Festival Karaez, Belgium's Dour, The T in the Park at Hamilton, in Scotland, Stratford's Phoenix – in Europe to keep the band's morale high. And wasn't the audience at Madrid's Revolver the most frenziedly enthusiastic to which any of them had ever played?

The anticipation of such a response made Charles playful. Before performing at the Parc Aquatica in Milan, he noticed his shirt was ripped, and patched it with a piece of duct (or gaffer) tape. Liking the way the patch looked, he kept sticking more and more of the silvery stuff on until the shirt was covered. Local fashion designers in the audience frantically designed the gaffawear collections that were the talk of the men's fashion world later that year.

In 1997, Charles and his band seemed to subscribe to the old adage that absence makes the heart grow fonder, and stayed out of audiences' sight – but only after one of the highest-profile performances of Charles' career, at David Bowie's 50th birthday show at Madison Square Garden, where he joined the great man for 'Fashion' (Bowie had apparently heard about Charles' having invented gaffawear, and yes, I *am* going to flog this one half to death) and 'Scary Monsters'.

A couple of months later, after playing a one-off concert in deepest Orange County and deciding to call his band Frank Black & The Catholics (The Jordanaires and The Inalienable Right to Eat Fred Astaire's Asshole were both taken, the latter by the group that became better known as The Butthole Surfers) headed into the studio to record a live demo of their next album. Charles was so pleased that he decided to issue it as-was. American Recordings kingpin Rick Rubin – who reckoned he knew a thing or two about hit records on the basis of his having been instrumental in the break-throughs of Run-DMC, The Beastie Boys, Public Enemy, and The Red Hot Chili Peppers – thought otherwise. Charles was taken aback when he learned that Marc Geiger, his most enthusiastic advocate at the label, was abandoning it.

Considerable to-ing and fro-ing commenced, almost certainly involving the invocation of the names of high-powered music biz attorneys. It was Ken Goes' impression that Rubin was going to let Charles offer the album for licensing to other labels, and then Ken Goes' impression that Rubin was going to do no such thing, and finally Ken Goes' impression that he'd never been involved in such maddening negotiations. In the end, Charles joined a label specialis-ing in excellent artists who no longer (or who never did) sell very well, most notably Richard Thompson. *Frank Black & The Catholics* wouldn't actually appear in British music stores until the following April, in American until June.

Throughout his career, Charles had demonstrated a remarkable penchant for shooting himself in the foot – here advertising for a rhythm section that liked Peter, Paul & Mary as well as Hüsker Dü, here ceasing, just as he launched his solo career, to use the stage name by which he'd become famous, everywhere being shamefully care-less with his lyrics. The decision to record his fourth album, *Frank Black & The Catholics*, hereinafter *The Orange Album*, direct-to-stereo (that is, without overdubbing) is very much in the tradition of those earlier decisions.

Not, of course, that the live approach doesn't have enormous appeal. As Charles himself explained, "What people do with technology is iron everything out, so everything's on 10 – as loud as it can be, as bright as it can be, as perfect as it can be. They're all trying to fit into a certain super tiny niche because of the rewards available to those that make it into the exclusive club of commercial radio. I don't listen to the radio. The music's too bland and there's just too much advertising. Most songs I hear today are over-produced. It's all the same. It could be a Top 10 hit or a dog food commercial. I can't tell. I have no interest in it at all."

Well, fair enough, and eloquently stated. But why does it have to be either indistinguishable from a dog food commercial or free of all overdubbing? Can there be no middle ground?

Raw and spontaneous, *The Orange Album*, as fans would come to call it, doesn't sound remotely like a dog food commercial. At its best, as on 'Solid Gold' or 'All My Ghosts', with Charles and Lyle unleashing great scorching gales of distortion on their respective stereo channels, it's thrilling. But how about the moment in the latter song when an obvious two- or more-part vocal "pad" comes in behind Charles' lead vocal, and it's just poor David McCaffrey, all on his lonesome? Would allowing him to have recorded a harmony part – or a few harmony parts – necessarily have stripped the song of its excitement?

Or how about the glorious cover of Larry Norman's (him again – the come on, pilgrim, man) fast country shuffle 'Six Sixty-Six'? There are a couple of places where Lyle is caught musically maybe not with his trousers down around his ankles, but at least with his fly open. Would the track be less hilarious if he'd been allowed to wipe the clumsy parts of the take we hear here and come up with something niftier?

We're deathly, deathly sick of excruciatingly perfect, lavishly fussed-over vocal tracks in the spring of 2004, as this is being written, and we were pretty fed up with them in 1998, when *The Orange Album* was released. But isn't there a vast middle ground between the sterile, prettified singing of perfumed pop singers and Charles' sounding, both here and on 'King & Queen Of Siam' and 'Suffering', like a drunken knobhead who's managed to wrest the microphone away from the lead singer at some poor pub band's gig?

In 'I Need Peace', Charles and Lyle briefly play a line in unison, and it sounds fab. What if, just to make it a bit beefier, they'd doubled it? Would the track have been stripped of all its power? No, it would have gained in it. The second half of Lyle's solo is marvellous, but I wouldn't bet against his wishing that he could have redone the first half.

If he had, would we wish we had a dog for which to buy Friskies?

On a couple of tracks, Scott Boutier is either using his crash cymbal as a ride (that is, beating eighth-notes on it rather than saving it for emphasis), or has taken his foot off his high-hat pedal. In a live context, that works wonderfully. On a recording, it's disastrous, as the track is suddenly awash in – opaque with – very high end. The drum entrance on 'The Man Who Was Too Loud' is almost comically quiet, making the moment far, far less exciting than it ought to have been. If all the instruments had been recorded separately, in the traditional way, Scott's entrance could have been brought up in the mix. Wouldn't that have made the track more, rather than less, effective?

If Charles were a novelist, would he allow his publisher access only to his first drafts on the assumption that later, improved drafts would lack spontaneity? If he were an actor (to a greater extent than he is [and the rest of us are] already, all the world being a stage), would he get his agent to stipulate contractually that the director not be allowed to use bits of different takes when assembling scenes in which Charles appears?

The impulse was noble but the actual idea not such a good one, not at all. In the end, it's yet another stupid pet trick.

All that said, 'Do You Feel Bad About It', on which his own guitar does most of the heavy lifting, represents a major breakthrough – Charles' first straightforward expression of his humanity, an angry, desperate appeal for a lover not to leave him. At last he takes as his text the oldest subject matter in the book, and it works a treat as he reveals himself . . . well, not too proud to beg.

Before they even met Kim, we pause to recall, Charles and Joey Santiago declared that their band would steer very clear of guitar solos. So why does Lyle Workman play one in nearly every song here? Only that on 'Solid Gold' will make the small hairs on many listeners necks stand to attention. If only Charles' lead vocal on the track weren't so affected.

'Suffering' has what might have been a great chorus – a hit single's chorus. Listening to this, one finds himself in the uncomfortable position of siding with the record company villain who thought a bit more production would be just the ticket. And once having admitted that, one might as well admit that few things on the album give him greater pleasure than the snippet of 'Green Acres Theme' with which it all begins. The boy (Lyle) can pick!

"If you just want garage punk, stripped of all the odd time signatures, subverted chord progressions, cryptic lyrics, and sonic experimentation that marked his first two albums, as well as his work with the Pixies, this album may satisfy your needs," groused Stephen Thomas Erlewine of *All Music Guide*, who neglected to specify what he meant by "subverted chord progression". (Ever noticed that rock writers are forever talking about chord progressions, but seem only in very rare instances actually to know what they are?)

But of course who am I to come on all high and mighty in the face of being unable to discern that, as Lyle Workman, a superior musician asserts, "Melodically, harmonically, rhythmically and sonically Frank Black is a true original. His music is complex without trying to be . . . His 'filter' [i e how he processes musical information] is very different from anyone else's."

Why, an online interviewer asked him in a chatroom, Frank Black & The Catholics and not just The Catholics? "Well, you know," said Charles with characteristic candour, "there's the ego to deal with."

Finally, two years after Lollapalooza, both Kelley, rehabilitated now in the eyes of the law, and Josephine Wiggs admitted they didn't want to be Breeders again, prompting the band's ever-philosophical sole remaining co-founder, Kim, to muse, "That was cool, but did they have to wait two fucking years to decide?" Kim realised that The Amps might as well call themselves The Breeders now. After a little-noticed solo project, *Go To The Sugar Altar*, Kelley came aboard, and they got a song onto the soundtrack of *The Mod Squad*.

After his band played a dozen California dates with John Doe, formerly of X, Charles flew to good old reliable France to plug his new album on three big radio shows. In May and June, he reunited with Lyle, Scott and David to play at a succession of clubs in the East, some in such heretofore-unvisited burgs as Sea Bright and Old Bridge, New Jersey, and Lancaster, Pennsylvania, not to mention Hungry Charley's nightclub in Syracuse. They were supported by lapsed Replacement Tommy Stinson's band Perfect, whose handsome young guitarist Dave Philips caught Charles' ear at the urging of Mr. Joseph A. Santiago.

As it began getting hot out, Pearl Jam invited the band to warm up some audiences for them. How could Charles say no after hearing that the tour would call in Rapid City, South Dakota, and East Troy, Wisconsin? Eddie and the boys were so delighted that they sneaked the Pixies' 'Monkey Gone To Heaven' and 'I've Been Tired' into performances in Denver, Portland, and Knoxville. It is not known for sure if Charles, who by this time was refusing even to speak his old band's name, heckled them viciously from the wings.

The Onion asked why there'd been so little sci-fi in his recent stuff. "I've avoided a lot of that in my more recent songwriting," he explained, "because I began seeing cartoon drawings of myself with an astronaut's helmet, or flying around in a spaceship – just corny shit like that."

But that turned out to have been the easy question. Charles now found himself having to explain a chance misogynistic-seeming remark he'd earlier made on MTV about girl rock singers maybe not being such a terrific idea. "[I] may have been reacting in part to the phenomenon of diary-rock, or whatever," he back-pedalled, "really shitty female vocalists who can't write songs, who are basically skating by on the fact that they have breasts and sing like babies."

White courtesy telephone for Kim Deal. Will Ms. Kim Deal please pick up the white courtesy telephone?

17

(Vicky's Story)
A Master of Everything

WHEN people hear that Alan and I visit Europe almost every summer, they swoon with envy. But it isn't nearly as glamorous and romantic as it sounds. Ours are very much working holidays – *gruelling* working holidays. In the past week, for instance, we've stayed more than one night in only one hotel, the Hotel Graf Moltke in Hamburg, and it wasn't exactly the Ritz. Given a choice between quantity and quality, Alan will choose the former every time. "We can afford five nights in three-star accommodation," he tells me, "or eight in two-star. Do the math."

So what if there weren't two pieces of furniture in our room in the Hotel Graf Moltke that bore even the slightest resemblance to one another? So what if the bed linen and towels all looked as though they'd been stolen from different bags left overnight in front of charity stores? So what if we were barely able to hear our own television if the one in the room to either side of us is on? So what if, when we left the hotel, we had to walk blocks through a neighbourhood popular with recent immigrants to Germany who, having not yet got their heads around the idea of indoor plumbing, peed blithely in the street, in plain view of all?

Trying to stretch our euros, we didn't actually do much during the day other than walk around looking at the menus of restaurants where Alan wouldn't consider actually eating, and comparison-shopping in whatever supermarkets we could find. When he was a child, his mom was apparently an implacable clipper of discount coupons, and he's very much her son. Only after we'd compared the prices of three items nearly every market could be counted on to have – Campbell's tomato soup, for instance, or Dr. Oetker's Big Americans pizza – in two different markets was Alan happy to buy our sandwich ingredients in the cheaper – provided it was cheaper than its rival on no fewer than four of the five items compared. If it was cheaper on only three, we'd go looking for Supermarket C, which in many instances took considerable finding. But really, what visitor to Hamburg wouldn't have preferred trying to find the Ananova nearest the Hotel Graf Moltke to seeing Harbour World Hamburg, say?

Yes, sarcasm.

After Hamburg, we paid our second visit to Paris. I still hadn't been to the Eiffel Tower, but I'd been to the Club Arapaho in Avenue d'Italie seven times (in seven nights, on our first visit, in '94), and that night I'd be seeing the Elysée Montmartre, as so many visitors to the Eiffel Tower or the Louvre hadn't.

Yes, more sarcasm.

But it could have been – and had been – far worse. Before we were married, Al went through a troubling stretch of Christian zealotry. You might have expected that to be a bridge too far for one who'd pretended, in his Do What Thou Wilt days, to worship Satan, but Al made the transition effortlessly. One day he was calling himself Aiwass, painting his fingernails black, and saying, when we couldn't figure out how we'd get the next month's rent paid, "Satan provides." The next day he'd discovered New Wave a decade or so after the fact, got himself a crew-cut, renamed himself Al E. Baster (correctly pronounced to rhyme with master, but commonly mispronounced to sound like something you'd use on a turkey, which is why he quickly abandoned it in exasperation and went back to Alan Jay Levine), and was asking me to tell anyone from the Wilts, if they phoned, that he wasn't in. He declared that "indie is where it's at", formed a new band that tried to look homeless (tried, that is, to look as though they'd nicked their wardrobe from the same carry-bags Hotel Graf Meltke had got its linen from) and sounded like Nirvana Jr, except with Christian themes, which he thought would ensure that they at least got a deal with a Christian label. When they didn't, he quit music in disgust and became obsessed with windsurfing, got bored with windsurfing and became obsessed with racing dirtbikes with his sort-of brother-in-law. Dennis and Tricia have three girls, and Den's the dotingest dad in Dedham.

Then, when we became the last household in North America to get online, Al discovered eBay. His sister had been doing well for herself, speaking of linens, buying at garage and estate sales up in Vermont and then selling them online. When Al discovered that people were selling everything under the sun on eBay, he offered a couple of rare English heavy metal albums from the early Seventies that he had multiple copies of from his days as a teenaged record plugger, and was flabbergasted when he found buyers almost immediately. He'd expected to make $25, wound up with $135, and was hooked again. The next thing I knew, he'd quit his job on the support line of a software programme that purported to double the storage capacity of Macintosh hard drives and become a dealer in regional rock memorabilia.

Other couples came to Europe for the pleasure of it. We came to Europe to attend as many performances by a particular artist — an artist Alan had decided had real staying power – as possible, to collect ticket stubs and document the performance in ridiculous detail for one of Al's several websites. It wasn't that he imagined he was going to get rich selling stubs from, say, The Dave Matthews Band's 1996 performances at the Arapaho immediately, but rather that they would slowly increase in value. It was, I was to understand, an investment. "Can you imagine if someone had thought to collect ticket stubs at the last scheduled Beatles performance, at Candlestick Park in the summer of 1966?" he'd ask with a faraway look in his eye. "They'd be set for life, man."

We were in Europe this time for Frank Black & The Catholics. I'd bought each of the Pixies albums on the day of their release, and had adored Frank's first two solo albums. *The Cult Of Ray* had left me a little cold, but then *The Orange Album*, the first on which the band was called the Catholics, got me loving him as much as I ever had. But six shows in the past six nights (at the Maria Am Ostbanhof in Berlin, Club Logo in Hamburg, Backstage in Munich, Cooky's in

Frankfurt, Zeche in Bochum, and Brussels' Botanique Gardens) had been quite enough. I felt as though I were watching a movie I loved on DVD over and over and over, or eating sushi (which had come to be my favourite food) for every meal.

I'd told Al when we were still over the Atlantic, en route from Boston, that I intended while in Paris to see the Eiffel Tower this time. Surely he could attend one performance on his own! But now that the hour was nigh, he pleaded with me to reconsider. It was far too much for one person, he insisted.

Five nights in a row we'd made sandwiches in our flea-bitten two-star hotel rooms with bread, cheese, lettuce, and so on we'd bought earlier in the day from the least expensive supermarkets in the environs of our hotels, or on trains. I proposed a deal: take me out to dinner and I'll go with you to the gig and see the Eiffel Tower next time. He agreed instantly. I should have asked for a real restaurant dinner two nights running.

We went down to the Left Bank, to the area I think they call St. Michel. Like Brussels, there were streets jam-packed with restaurants, except the ones in Brussels had all seemed to offer very similar menus, whereas you could get just about anything you wanted here – Greek, Italian, Chinese, Thai, Indian, even Indian – and every last one of them had your best friend in the world standing out in front. Which is to say that, just like the girls we'd seen shivering and tottering in front of topless/bottomless bars on San Francisco's Broadway, rasping at us in their cigarette-ruined voices to come in – absolutely free! – for a look at the girls, there was an invariably stocky, swarthy guy in front of every restaurant trying to guess the nationalities of passers-by and begging them to accept vouchers entitling them to free drinks or desserts.

It was unnerving how they all knew, without Al and I exchanging a syllable in their hearing, that we were English speakers, as I'd have preferred to imagine that my nationality wasn't that transparent. The worst were those with conversational gambits. They'd beam rapturously as you approached and say, "Hungry? Most delicious cuisine in all the Left Bank inside." If you smirked at them, they'd pretend to try to guess where you were from. "From London?" they'd say. "New York, New York? Chicago? Newcastle? I have a cousin there."

"A cousin where, bro?" Al, amused, couldn't help but ask one of them in front of a Greek place offering a fixed price menu for €12,20. "You mentioned four different places."

"All of them, my very good friend," the restaurant dude claimed, beaming, forcing a voucher into Al's hand. "I have many cousins. And you, my very good friend – and your lovely young companion – have a delicious meal ahead of you. What do you like? Meat? Fish? Our chef is a master of everything."

How was one supposed to resist *that*? Not that we didn't try. I told the guy we'd only just finished our late lunch, but might be back later. He gave me the look he'd have given a doctor who'd just come out to say that his nine-year-old daughter had died on the operating table.

We walked around some more, knowing better now than even to smile at any of the restaurant pimps. Al wanted to go to a Chinese place with a €10,90 fixed-price menu, but the few diners inside looked sullen, and I wasn't in the mood for Chinese anyway. I asked how, for barely more than a euro more, he could resist a place whose chef was the master of everything. The look on his face told me he had serious reservations about spending more than we had to on this, our splurge night, but he shrugged and sighed and acceded.

I'd expected our very good friend of many cousins in front of the Greek place to be overjoyed at our return, but he acted as though he'd fully expected it, and the free drink to which my voucher entitled me turned out to be enough very sweet wine to drown a small cockroach in, but just barely. Judging from the looks on their faces, none of those our very good friend of many cousins had seduced earlier seemed to agree about the chef's range of mastery. My starter suggested, for instance, that he had not yet mastered *taramasalata*. Of course, I had to pretend that I found it all inexpressibly delicious, even while Al glowered resentfully at his *pastitsio*.

We were seated right out in the front window, and I think our very good friend of many cousins was worried other suckers might see his face and not allow themselves to be seduced, so he actually asked Alan if his dinner were all right. "To be honest, bro," Alan said, trying to incinerate the dish with his glare, "it sucks."

Our host sighed. "It is easy to find good chefs, but impossible to keep them. They are with you two nights. Then the place round the corner offers them a few euros more and *poof*, they are vanished." He wondered if Alan might like to try something else instead. Alan said nearly anything would be an improvement. The guy sighed again, and removed the *pastitsio*, returning a moment later with *moussaka*. "I feel sure you will enjoy this, my friend," he sighed, and went back outside before Alan could tell him he didn't.

"Well," I lied, "*mine* was delicious."

Al pronounced his *moussaka* "better than the *pastitsio*, but that isn't saying very much." He looked as he ate it – and there would be no doubt of his eating every morsel of it, considering that he'd have to pay for it – like a little boy given a choice between finishing his dinner and having his PlayStation sent to a more deserving little boy in Somalia or something. But then he brightened for some reason at the sight of our very good friend of many cousins trying to lower the boom on a nondescript guy in a backwards Red Sox cap and a very American-looking woman in a Nantucket T-shirt and shorts. "Look who our friend found in his net," he laughed delightedly.

"Who?" I said.

"Don't you recognise him?"

I have rotten vision, and didn't. I ought to wear reading glasses on top of my contact lenses for close work, but I'm too vain, and asked my optometrist to sacrifice a little of my distance vision so I could read without additional help.

"It's Scott," Alan said, amazed that I could fail to recognise a celebrity of such standing, "the drummer, the Catholics' drummer!"

"Wow," I said, with a hint of irony that Alan didn't detect. He was too busy trying to figure out if there was a way he might be able to parlay this chance sighting into something eBay users would want to bid on. He abruptly got up and hurried out to them. He said something that made Scott furrow his brow thoughtfully. Scott and his companion tried to give back our very good friend of many cousins' vouchers. Our friend of many cousins scowled. Scott and his companion walked on. Alan said something to our friend of many cousins, who seemed not to regard Alan with the same affection as before.

Alan came back in. "Well," he said, "after all these years, now we're even. You saved Black Francis' guitarist from having his hand broken, and now I've saved Frank Black's drummer from a really lousy meal."

He was teasing. When we first started going out, maybe six months after I brought Dennis and his friend to Worcester to keep Alan's knucklehead friends away from Joey Santiago, one of the first things I asked (after "Don't you feel a little silly looking like that and playing such old-fashioned music") was whether he'd really have gone through with his plan to stop Joey playing the guitar. He just burst into laughter, thinking it hilarious that I'd have imagined him capable of such a thing. Didn't I realise that the whole Satanism thing had been just an attempt to try to look sexier and more exotic? He'd never hurt a fly, let alone a Filipino – and oh, how he roared with self-delight when *that* popped out. The knuckleheads at the Worcester gig had been just a couple of old school friends with whom he knew he and Tony (then Anton) could get a lift. (He hadn't yet passed his driving test, and Anton's licence had been suspended for too many moving violations.) It may well have been that Anton, whom he got a lot of pleasure from putting on, seriously disdained the Pixies, but Alan himself had loved them from their first show at the Rat. How could I have imagined that he'd devote a whole evening to driving to Worcester to see a band he didn't really like?

And I'd thought Tiffani Cohen (now a paediatrician, by the way – and the one to whom Tricia and Dennis take their daughters) had no sense of irony.

We made our way to the gig. Elysée Montmartre sounded pretty swanky, but it was just another medium-sized club choking in cigarette smoke – the French do so love their Gîtanes. I went in and got a table while Alan worked the door, trying to get people to give him their ticket stubs, asking if they had any interesting Frank Black stuff they wanted to sell or trade. I couldn't imagine that anyone who didn't speak English understood him, as he'd learned all his French from books, but had skipped the pronunciation part, and pronounced everything as it would have been pronounced in English.

I couldn't help but worry about him. In Munich, he'd just about got himself walloped. A couple of ticket scalpers had supposed that he was trying to hawk tickets of his own, and gave him a talking-to – in German, which neither of us speaks a syllable of. If a bilingual Frank fan hadn't intervened, God knows what might have become of him. The home-grown scalpers' faces had suggested they weren't strangers to knife fights.

My principal jobs were to make note of what the band performed, and which instrument Rich Gilbert played. I also had to time each song with the stopwatch function of my Casio wristwatch. Some of Frank's more obsessive fans were interested to know where, for instance, the longest and shortest versions of 'Hermaphroditos' had been performed, as well as every syllable Frank uttered between songs, and what, if not his usual black 501s and Stussy T-shirt, he'd been wearing.

When we had to fly home, one of Al's several partner webmasters would attend the shows in our place, making their own detailed notes. The important thing was that every performance be extensively documented by somebody. Al felt maintaining a website containing information that fans couldn't get anywhere else served to enhance his collectible business. Indeed, a huge majority of his eBay customers had first heard of him by way of *frankblackminutaie.com*. (Thinking that only a small minority of the most literate can actually spell *minutiae*, I'd urged him to name it something else, but he'd gone ahead. It was my opinion that Google had saved his bacon.)

Once the support band started, Al scurried to try to get somebody at the venue to tell him exactly how many people were present. His was no longer the only fansite that specified how many people were at every show, so he'd had to think of something new, and had decided that he would say how many persons of colour were at the shows we saw. Not that many persons of colour seemed very interested in Frank, but a lot more in France and Germany than in America. Not that it was always easy to determine if a person should be classed as one thing or the other. Al had told me that if a person of indeterminate ethnicity moved fluidly in time to the music, he would count them as a person of colour.

It was quite a good performance, the one after our big splurge dinner, but its overfamiliarity made my mind wander. I nonetheless scribbled no fewer than four pages of notes in my steno notebook.

I'd never admit it to Alan, but I actually looked forward to getting home and back to my third graders.

Afterwards, we needed to get back to our two-star hotel (in a neck of the woods in which it was Africans peeing unashamedly in the street) promptly to get a good night's sleep before leaving the next morning for Rennes, at whose Ubu Club we would see one more show before flying home. But a couple of guys in leather jackets and watch caps stopped us halfway to the Metro. They hadn't been in knife fights, or at least any that had left scars, but I still looked around anxiously, hoping for passers-by who could intervene if we needed them.

"I think you have the Frank Black minutiae website," the one with the floppy Hugh Grant hair and eyes that went in slightly different directions accused Alan in an accent that had him not thinking, but sinking. I inched backwards, giving myself room if I had to try to kick him.

"What about it, dude?" Al, a firm believer in not showing fear, challenged him.

Floppy Hair made that weird sound of disdain the French are so good at, sort of half raspberry, half *hrr* "It is bullshit," he said. "I was at one of the shows at the Arapaho seven years ago. You – how you say? – got the order of the songs wrong. And you said Frank did 'Places Named After Numbers'. That is bullshit, *monsieur*."

He sure loved saying *bullshit*, this guy, and sure said it cutely. *Bullsheet* – that which Ferdinand has on his bed. His friend, apparently lacking comparable fluency in English, merely glared.

"There were several shows," Alan said, not giving an inch. "Maybe we were at different ones."

"I was at all six," his accuser snarled.

"Ah," Al, who could be very sarcastic when he chose to be, said, "but there were actually seven in all."

"Bullshit," the guy said yet again, and spat. *Bullsheet*. "You Americans do not appreciate genius."

18

Crankin' Them Amps

IT'S very possible – and, indeed, believed by many – that Charles performed 'Nimrod's Son' at the House of Blues in Hollywood on the evening of June 24, 1999, the first time he'd played a Pixies song publicly since quitting the stage of Vancouver's Commodore Ballroom on the evening of April 25, 1992. What's known for sure is that he and his band toured through January, making their first appearances at such hot spots as the Orangutan in Gulfport, Mississippi, the Covered Dish in Gainesville, and Juanita's Cantina Ballroom in Little Rock, where there is no evidence of their having gone out for hush puppies and pussy with Bill Clinton, whose tastes are known to have run more to Fleetwood Mac and Barbra Streisand. Charles submitted to an interview in Atlanta with the animated (in the Disney sense) namesake of the Cartoon Network's *Space Ghost Coast To Coast*, but it was never aired. Conspiracy? Draw your own conclusions.

Once having played Stubb's Barbeque in Austin a couple of weeks before Valentine's Day, they allowed themselves a break, and then headed in mid-April to Scandinavia and good old reliable Western Europe, this time including Luxembourg. In London, their agent for Europe, who would later explain, "People are prepared to put up with 20 Frank Black & The Catholic songs to hear five Pixies songs," (and note his interesting choice of "put up with" to describe how audiences responded to the Frank Black material), presumably rubbed his hands together with glee.

June and July found them back in the USA, and performing at

such venues as the Higher Ground in Winooski, Vermont, the Holy Cow in Salt Lake City, and Gabe's Oasis in Iowa City, Iowa, the latter the venue to which young Midwestern performing artists aspire as fervently as young Easterners used to aspire to Carnegie Hall, and yes, we're just being snide again, even while our poor old heart goes out to them. *Gigantic* has itself performed in places like Gabe's Oasis, and had locals come up between original songs and ask if we couldn't play something by Santana instead.

"You learn," Charles was overheard to sigh, "where the good cafés and truck stops are. You learn to love certain stretches of road just for the sheer beauty of it. And, of course, the big payoff at the end of most days is the gig.

"We get to play – that's a great reward, getting to play at a rock show. I mean, that never gets boring. There's always something exciting about it, whether it's sold out or not, whether it's a big club or a tiny club, whether it's a great place or a shitty place. The bottom line is that you're going to play music and there are going to be people there to hear you. It's exciting to go out there and prove yourself, to go out there and say, 'I have a great rock moment in me, so stick around for a while.'

"Not to brag or anything, but we can sell a few tickets in Paris, France, on a Friday night and fill a 3,000-seat theatre. Other nights, you're playing in a microbrewery with waitresses yelling at you because people are still eating – these humbling little experiences. But it's great. It's the life of a professional musician."

In the autumn, Charles lay low, finally coming out of hibernation to perform first at the Sweet Relief Musicians Fund Concert in LA, and then a few days later, with the satirist Roy Zimmerman at good old reliable McCabe's. The two wacky tunesmiths took turns playing their songs until the end of the show, when they both sang original songs at the same time, shenanigans perhaps inspired by The Velvet Underground.

He released a new album, *Pistolero*, about which the loyal *Nude As The News* hyperbolised, "[It] posits Frank Black in a Neil Young-esque role, writing and rocking for the sake of the music, tirelessly wrenching powerful sounds from the gut of his guitar and offering them in homage to the altar of Rock'n'Roll. He's still got luscious hooks and melodies, but no frills. While his words are still eccentric [keep a dictionary close at hand], Black has discarded most of the musical complicity [sic] of his past in favour of a simple and direct approach that appeals more to the heart of rock than its mind. Listen hard – you'll feel it."

Gigantic didn't, finding *Pistolero* all punked-out roar and no substance, and pretty nearly unlistenable. (Behold the awful vengeance of [producer] Nick Vincent, former [apparently *very* reluctant, though the pay probably exceeded Charles'] Donny 'n' Marie sideman.) It sounds as though Charles must have got an endorsement deal with a different – and inferior – amplifier manufacturer or something. The distortion of the guitars on *The Orange Album* was noticeably richer and smoother.

"I don't record everything every step of the way," Charles told an interviewer who asked about his songwriting around this time. "I just pick up my guitar and try to come up with a song. I don't write anything down, I just try to remember everything in my head. I assume that weeds out the mediocre ideas, and that it's the good stuff I'll remember."

Guess again, bro. It's the very, very low quality of the songwriting that's the main problem on this virtually tuneless grunge-a-thon. Charles' musical policy seems to have been reduced to: crank the amps and no one will notice that the song's crap. Punk's not dead (here with the oft-omitted apostrophe), but the likes of 'So Hard To Make Things Out', over five minutes of grinding ugly tedium, are more than enough to make you wish otherwise.

'Bad Harmony' isn't, as you might hope, about Kim Deal, though Charles uses it as a pretext for some vengeful screaming. His fascination with the notion of somnambulism in '85 Weeks' is only slightly less annoying than his earlier fascination, back on *Trompe Le Monde*, with Jefrey Feld's odd spelling of Jefrey. 'Billy Radcliffe' is similarly whimsical, but tuneless. If we have learned nothing else from Ray Davies, isn't it that whimsy must be whistle-able?

New boy Rich Gilbert, whom Charles had known since the early Pixies days in Boston, when Rich was one of The Zulus, does his best. He plays some exuberantly crazy lead guitar on the album's

A poorly executed artsy-type shot in which Joey looks unlike both himself and Matthew Broderick. *(LFI)*

Charles lets fly a bloodcurdling scream on stage at the Pukkelpop Festival, August 25, 1991. *(LFI)*

Joey at the Brixton Academy, June 26, 1991. *(Steve Double/Retna)*

Kim at the Brixton Academy, June 26, 1991. *(Steve Double/Retna)*

Charles indicates how big he intends to become as a solo artist, January 20, 1993. But it was not to be! *(Paul Bergen/Redferns)*

Frank Black solo at Electric Ladyland, June 24, 1993. *(Steve Eichner/WireImage)*

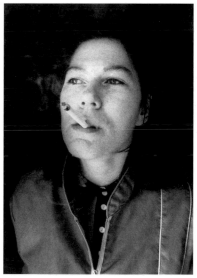

Kim in 1995, brazenly disregarding health warnings. Rock and roll! *(SIN/Corbis)*

Charles got all dressed up to perform live with David Bowie at the still-ambulatory old rascal's 50th birthday celebration concert Madison Square Garden, NYC, January 9, 1997. *(Kevin Mazur/WireImage)*

Charles backstage at the Reading Festival, August 2001, looking for all the world like a minder or Chelsea supporter. *(David Atlas/Retna)*

Charles DJs at the Barfly in London, June 21, 2003. *(Jeff Davy/Retna)*

Frank Black with the Catholics, 2003. Rich Gilbert wears glasses. *(Ian Dickson/Redferns)*

Backstage with Bowie, Martin Gore and Perry Farrell after Bowie's Reality Tour performance of February 2, 2004. *(Lester Cohen/WireImage)*

The reunited Pixies hold a rare press conference on Day 1 of the Coachella Festival, Indo, California, May 1, 2004, Charles looking unnervingly like the late Divine.
(Kelly A. Swift/Retna)

David Lovering on stage at T in the Park, July 10, 2004. *(LFI)*

Charles on stage in Berlin, June 29, 2004. *(LFI)*

Joey on stage in California, April 29, 2004. *(LFI)*

Kim, a rather bigger Deal than in the group's original incarnation, on stage at the Pinkpop fest, Holland, May 30, 2004. *(LFI)*

None dares call him Chuck! *(Chapman Baehler/Retna)*

highlight, the thrilling, terrifying, anarchic 'I Switched You'. Joey Who? On the album-closing 'So. Bay' he manages the best imitation you'll ever hear of George Harrison played backwards. He plays pedal steel on the otherwise not-notable 'You're Such A Wire', and joins poor David McCaffrey on background vocals, but not terribly robustly.

Even the cover art's rubbish again. This direct-to-stereo lark isn't working, Charles, and neither is imagining that attitude is all.

"I love Charles to death," Gil Norton was heard to sigh in suburban north London when asked why they no longer worked together, "but he has this . . . obsession for live-to-two-track."

NME bewailed Charles' "juvenile belief in strangled melodies and the 'charm' of the three-chord trick, which, when stretched over 14 turbulent tracks, ultimately grates . . . Faux-naïve reflections are scattered over a soundtrack of dumb guitars and primal drumming. *Pistolero* is an old-skool garage-rock album: loud, lumbering, graceless, and intermittently great fun."

"This," Charles acknowledged, "is the second record I have recorded live-to-two-track, which I am very proud of – perhaps too proud. I mean, who cares how I recorded it? Either it's good or it stinks." Well, no. Maybe one of the reasons it stinks, to whatever extent it may be said to stink, is *because* of how you recorded it.

New millennium, same old cruddy club circuit. Shortly after Valentine's Day, Charles and band headed for the Midwest, where they managed a rare performing visit to Sioux Falls, South Dakota. Mere days later, they were in Boise, Idaho. Oh, the glamour!

"I'm not cynical or angry," Charles, ever the good sport about this sort of thing, assured another interviewer. "I don't have to struggle to earn a living. I'm basically a liquor and beer salesman – you know, selling drinks in bars to patrons. The next step up is to be a ticket salesman for theatre owners, making money for them and the unions – and me, of course." He didn't mention that it hadn't been so many years since he had indeed been a pretty prolific ticket salesman for theatre owners – or, at least, concert promoters. He didn't need to.

After a bunch of Southern California dates, the band spent a couple of weeks recording their *Dog In The Sand* album, on which they bravely remained one of the few established acts in the world on whose recordings Eric Clapton had not made a guest appearance, this in spite of talk of slipping Mississippi blues forefather Son House's 'John The Revelator' into their live repertoire. Instead, continuing the proud tradition of drafting members of former opening acts, they got Dave Philips, earlier of Perfect – and before that a member of Jack Logan & The Liquor Cabinet, which hadn't put Athens, Georgia, on the map to quite the extent R.E.M. had.

The album's title track was said to have been recorded at 4.30 in the morning. Indeed, Charles characterised the whole album as "a very wee hours kind of record". It turned out that the singing lessons he'd been taking from a Los Angeles opera singer to try to ensure that he'd remain able to hit all his high notes after the first few nights of a tour had served to make him able to sing all night if he chose to.

His fans believed that while on tour, their hero had listened to a lot of late Sixties and early Seventies Stones and Dylan. The very 'Brown Sugar'-ish 'Blast Off' and the 'Gimme Shelter'-aping 'My Name Is Hermaphroditos' – and most of all 'I've Seen Your Picture', in which he performs the best Mick Jagger vocal imitation you will hear in your lifetime, or in your children's – strongly suggest corroboration of the one, if not the other. With two more musicians – the returned Eric (no longer Drew) Feldman and alternate lead guitarist Dave Philips – on everything, and Feldman's old pal Moris Tepper making a couple of cameos, there's an awful lot of good musicianship deployed in the service of another programme of mostly tuneless, lyrically impenetrable crapola.

As big an influence as the Stones are on the three tracks named above, it's the influence of the sublime Robyn Hitchcock that most informs what for *Gigantic* is the album's not-exactly-stratospheric highlight, 'St. Francis Dam Disaster', in which Charles relates the poignant tale of some heretofore dammed water making its (her!) way across southern California to be with lots of its (her!) own kind at the coast. The dead give-away that this isn't a Hitchcock cover being that it's pretty well devoid of melodic interest.

It's been said that there really isn't such a thing as an unenjoyable pizza. In much the same way, there's no such thing as an unevocative pedal steel guitar. Rich Gilbert plays his with considerable panache, nowhere more notably than on 'Stupid Me', on which he makes it sigh gorgeously. If only the song's actual melody were half so evocative. Whose idea was it to bring back the Gary Smith snare drum sound for this track?

Over and over here, we have the playing far, far exceeding that which is being played.

In 'I'll Be Blue', Charles ventures into Elvis Costello territory. But again he's neglected to come up with a tune, and his singing is just plain awful – really rotten intonation doth not expressiveness make. 'Llano del Rio' has some appealing word play ("If you really want to/ You can practise Esperanto") but no tune, and goes on and on and on at the end. Retroactive memo to (producer) Mr. Nick Vincent: Hit *Stop* for Christ's sake, will you please, bro?

The sombre, leaden title track doesn't benefit at all from having so many musicians playing on it, Dave Philips' strumming along with the drums seeming especially superfluous. If they hadn't recorded direct-to-stereo, they might have reconsidered his participation and taken it out before the album was sent to Mr. Eddy Schreyer for mastering. But oh, no.

"*Dog*," wrote the implacably sycophantic *Nude As The News*, "brings to mind the purity of American music as it's experienced driving a car through the vast expanses of the Southwest plains. *Dog In The Sand* isn't going to launch any revolutions or kick-start any more young Cobains, but it's nevertheless a lovely slice of music."

"The trademark wit and weirdness is back," wrote Gareth Grundy in one of the glossy British music monthlies, leading some to wonder why he hadn't used *are*. The *Guardian* noted that "The title track is an incredible song, and 'Bullet' – a loopy, spaghetti Western-inflected trill screwing together Santiago's distinctive squeal and Black's equally idiosyncratic obsession with little green aliens – is utterly blissful. But both tracks were written before the death of the Pixies."

19

(Vicky's Story)
His Own Little Corner of Hell

I CHOSE to teach third grade because that's when kids really begin to reveal who they are to the world. Their parents have probably known for years, but it typically isn't until around age seven that most children realise they don't have to keep putting on the brave face they've maintained through second grade. At seven and eight, you can already tell which kids are going to bully and which be bullied, and so on. What I really hoped to do when I decided to become a teacher was see if I could alter the course of those kids who appeared headed for disaster.

I've thought an awful lot about bullying and decided that all bullied children the world over have one thing in common – they allow it. Maybe it's genetic, and maybe a function of their parents modelling the wrong responses. I have often thought, given my dad's passivity, that I was lucky, to whatever microscopic sense I could have said to have been lucky as a lonely, persecuted child, not to have been a boy. If I'd taken the passivity I'd learned from my dad to my primary school, Jonny McWilliams, the class sociopath, would surely have had me as a late breakfast every morning.

There's a boy called Will among my current third graders, and another called Karl. Will is bright, gentle, absurdly good-looking, very sensitive and, because of the sensitivity, a huge favourite of Karl, the biker's son, who, at seven, is already voraciously furious at the world. Karl will eagerly seize any opportunity to belittle Will, in language that would singe a longshoreman's eyebrows, and has beaten him up twice already this semester.

When he finally (after multiple invitations) came in to confer with me and Mr. Coleman, the school principal, and Mrs. Hernandez, the school district psychologist, Karl's dad pretty much laughed with delight in our faces when we told him what had been going on. "It's never too early to learn to use the fists that God gave you, is it?" he asked Mr. Coleman, slapping his knee, reeking of sweat and leather.

When I or Mrs. Hernandez or Will's mom addressed him, he kept his eyes firmly on Mr. Coleman as he answered – in those cases where he deigned to answer at all. My impression was that he wasn't about to be seen talking to a woman, unless as part of sexual preda-tion. And the really infuriating part was that Mr. Coleman, who, back in his own childhood, was almost certainly Will, some Jonny McWilliams' patsy, was palpably flattered by these intimations of shared *machismo*.

I know it's very wrong of me to want to march Karl into the boys' room and drown him in one of the sinks, but that's exactly what I do feel at times, mostly, I suppose, because up to age 12 or so, I was very much Will. I was bigger than nearly everyone in my class, but that only made things worse for me – sadistic children love nothing more than brutalising classmates larger than themselves. Finally, as you know, when I did begin using my feet and fists, it only got me per-ceived as a freak. I was damned if I did, and damned if I didn't. Sometimes, seeing in Karl the boys who made my own childhood so miserable, I really do want to get my hands around his scrawny little neck and squeeze until he ceases to struggle. And he a seven-year-old boy.

But as the Jesuits say, "Give me a child to the age of seven and I have that person for life." Which means that there already might be no hope for this poor, battered little boy anymore, and that, however fervently we might wish otherwise, allowing him to remain in society will be to everyone's great detriment, as it is already to Will's. Karl can't respond to kindness. He only sneers at it, his little face a startling mask of contempt. And I know from bitter experience that Will hears every last taunt, and hates himself for enduring it. Karl's tragedy becomes Will's. As the one expresses his bottomless anger, the other's self-respect is eroded.

All this on my mind, and Al waiting for me at home, pacing maniacally, smacking his lips, making that maddening sucking noise – but not hearing voices.

Less than a month before we got home from our last visit to Europe, he began finding it really difficult to sleep. I'd wake up at three in the morning and find myself alone in bed. He'd be out in the living room glaring at his monitor, furious at some minuscule fragment of misinformation about Frank Black he'd found on somebody else's website. But far better that than the night about 10 days later when I found him in the living room at almost 4 o'clock curled foetally and shivering in the middle of the room, terrified by something I couldn't perceive.

"Can't you hear them?" he demanded when I asked what was wrong.

I could hear only the sound of a distant car on the wet street. When I told Al, he gave me a look that chilled the blood in my arteries – a look of the most savage contempt. "You're telling me you can't hear the voices?" he demanded. They were male voices, apparently whispering, but whispering quite audibly. They told him his work was bullshit. They said they were going to get him, and crush his hands.

For a millisecond, I wanted to ask how they pronounced *bullshit*, or what good crushing his hands would do when he wasn't a Filipino, or even a guitarist. But it was obvious – terrifyingly so – that he wasn't fooling around.

I eventually was able to persuade him to come back to bed with me, but the next night I woke up and realised he was gone again. He was in the living room, this time standing in front of the silent, blank television with his Bruins hockey stick raised. "When they come," he explained, "they'll probably come through there, but I'll be ready for them."

I made an emergency appointment for him to see a doctor the next day. The doctor thought the situation serious enough to get him a same-day referral with a shrink, who in turn got him admitted to the hospital for 72 hours' observation. I was absolutely frightened to death, and couldn't keep myself from wondering how I might have helped bring it on.

The psychiatrist's diagnosis was acute schizophrenia. He'd started Al on a medication – an atypical antipsychotic – called risperidone, which often was very successful in suppressing the sorts of symptoms Al was . . . presenting. He wanted to keep him under observation for three more days.

When Al came home, he wasn't hearing voices condemning his website, but feeling light-headed and dizzy. He hadn't been able to budge his bowels in three days, and his vision was slightly blurred. "Wow," I managed to say, trying to put the best face on it, "it's almost like you're in love." We laughed together, hollowly.

After about a week, he began doing weird things with his face – smacking his lips, chewing, sucking, twisting his tongue. I phoned the doctor, who sounded inconvenienced and told me these behaviours were known collectively as *tardive dyskinesia*, seen in lots of people on risperidone. I asked if it would stop. He said there was no way of knowing. I told him Al was now officially chronically constipated. He called that the *anticholinergic effect*, and said it was no less common than the other symptoms. Smug bastard, smug jargon spewing bastard. It was his neck I wanted to get my hands around. I resolved not to phone him again if I didn't have to.

When Al became too jittery to sit down for more than a minute or two at a time, I got online and discovered the condition was called *akathisia*. Not having had to consult Dr Pompous to find that out didn't make it much easier for me to watch Al, who had pretty clearly come to inhabit his own little corner of Hell.

We ceased, of course, to have sex. I'd always been able to get him interested by getting slutted out, as we called it, putting my makeup (very pale foundation, lavishly outlined eyes, blindingly red lips) on with a trowel, and wearing an outfit I wore in public only at Halloween each year – a very short leather skirt, fishnet stockings, fingerless fishnet gloves, huge hoop earrings, stiletto-heeled ankle boots, and a huge Tina Turner wig. Al had been so excited by the whole idea the first year he saw it that we never made it to the Halloween party. He found it very sexy for me to play all the lurid little groupies he'd never had.

In time, after we effectively stopped making love unless I was in my Halloween outfit, I told him I felt objectified, as though it were the wig and costume he was making love to rather than me. He said that male arousal had a lot more to do with visual stimuli than female, and that he could hardly help being male. There was a reason street-walkers dressed as they did, he pointed out – to enflame prospective patrons. Why, he wondered, would I be content to get him four aroused on a scale of one to 10 when in my groupie get-up I rarely failed to get him 12?

But now, as the medication kicked in, not even the promise of seeing me spectacularly slutted out seemed to interest him. Every time I broached the subject, he said, "Maybe tomorrow night. I'm too groggy to enjoy it at the moment."

One night I didn't ask him first, but just put the whole outfit on while he watched TV. I leaned back against the wall behind him with one foot up, as though posing for the cover of an early Sixties detective novel or something, and said, "Any rock stars around here interested in having their cocks sucked?"

His look of terror and confusion when he noticed me was absolutely heartbreaking. The last thing I'd wanted was to make him feel bad. I was gigantically relieved when he remembered the drill, and a delighted leer spread over his face. As far as I knew, he hadn't been erect in weeks, but he finally managed it. He tried to get me to come over to him, but I gave him the sort of sneer I knew he found terribly sexy and headed for the bedroom.

He hurried after me, gasping with lust. "I've bought all your albums," I said, touching it lightly with my fingertip, making him shiver with excitement, "and bought a ticket to see you every time your group has played this city." I knelt. I swallowed him. He moaned.

I was at it forever, until my jaw began to ache. He abruptly stepped away. "I don't know what's wrong," he said.

I couldn't let him go there, not even for a second. "Nothing," I said, "that a little of this won't fix." I unzipped my skirt, letting it fall around my feet, revealing that I wore no panties. I regained his interest. I lay back on the bed. He entered me. It was working. Everything was going to be fine. In fact, we seemed to be going at it much longer than usual.

And then it wasn't working either and he withdrew, sobbing, "I can't finish."

"There's no hurry, is there? Take your time. I was enjoying it."

"Fuck," he said. "Fuck, fuck, fuck. I *wasn't* enjoying it. I was right on the verge for a couple of minutes both times, but I couldn't pull the trigger. It was fucking torture."

"It happens," I said, though I had no reason to believe it.

"No, it doesn't. Not being able to get it up happens. Not being able to finish *doesn't* happen, not unless you're taking something that *makes* it not happen. Like that fucking risperidone. Oh, God, Vicky, what's going to become of me? I'm 31 years old and I'll never be able to enjoy sex again?"

"Of course you'll enjoy sex again, Al. Of course you will. This is just temporary. You'll see." But I wasn't so sure. And I'd be lying if I said it didn't occur to me that staying with him might mean my own sex life was over at 29.

A couple of weeks after our sex life ended, Al came back from his semi-weekly medical check-up and announced he'd gained four pounds. I'd thought I might have seen his chin beginning to double, but had been able to pretend I hadn't. In doing my earlier research, I'd seen that something like 60 per cent of those taking atypical antipsychotics gain weight. Al had always been proud of his body. He lifted weights when we watched TV. At one point, we'd jogged together at least five nights a week.

"This is unacceptable," he called from the bathroom, where he'd gone to examine himself shirtless in the mirror, "completely fucking unacceptable."

I went in to him, and put my arms around his waist (while I still could, I thought, in spite of myself). "Is it less acceptable," I said, "than the voices in your head?

"Don't worry, babe," I continued. "All it means is that there's more of you to love."

At school, Wayne, one of the 5th grade alpha males, decided to appoint himself Will's protector, apparently just to be contrary. Twenty-four hours earlier, there'd been no more voracious a persecutor of our weak and defenceless than Wayne himself. But his self-appointment didn't become widely known until the afternoon he broke Karl's nose.

When brought in to explain himself to Mr. Coleman, he said, "Well, somebody's got to stand up for the weak and defenceless, don't they?" with such smouldering self-righteousness that we might have burst into laughter if we hadn't been so close to tears.

When Mr. Coleman asked Will to corroborate Wayne's story that he'd offered Wayne $10 to frighten Karl, we all noticed the intimidating look Wayne gave Will. When we asked Wayne to wait in another office, Will tearfully denied the whole thing. "Where was I supposed to get that kind of money?" he whimpered, almost more adorably than I could bear.

Karl's dad showed up shortly thereafter, reeking not only of sweat and leather this time, but of beer too, and this in mid-afternoon. "Who did this to you, boy?" he demanded when we led him in to Karl, who was holding ice to his nose in the nurse's office, "and what did you do back?"

Karl looked at me, as though for help. I never imagined I'd see the day. "I asked you a question, boy," his dad growled.

"Why don't we give the boy a few more minutes to . . ." Mr. Coleman began.

"Shut it," Karl's dad, no longer Mr. Coleman's good buddy, no longer half of that duo of bonded males, snarled, giving Mr. Coleman a look I hope nobody ever gives me. He turned back to Karl. "If I hear you didn't kick his ass across the goddamn playground, mister, you're in a world of trouble when you get home. Count on it."

"Did he?" Karl's dad demanded back in Mr. Coleman's office. "Did he kick the little son-of-a-bitch's goddamn face in?"

"His assailant was a fifth grader," Mr. Coleman began to explain, "considerably bigger than . . ."

"I don't give a flying fuck at a donut if he's a lineman for the fucking Patriots," Karl's dad interrupted. "If Karl didn't find a way to hurt him, he's in *mucho, mucho* deep shit. And he knows it."

Everyone looked at his or her own lap. "Give me a name," Karl's dad demanded. "If Karl didn't do it himself, I'll have to do it for him. Give me an address. I touch a fifth grader, they'll throw me back in the can. But you can bet I'll take it up big time with the fifth grader's old man. Give me an address."

"I'm afraid that's quite impossible," Mr. Coleman said, looking very, very pale, and sounding it.

Karl's dad farted loudly without apology or even comment as he seemed to consider trying to force the information he wanted out of Mr. Coleman. There was a time when I might have taken him on myself, but age had made me circumspect. He didn't seem the sort to pull punches just because it was a woman's face he was punching.

There was a timid little knock on the door of Mr. Coleman's office. I had only to lean over to open it. It was Will, with tears streaming down his perfect golden cheeks, holding his surprisingly non-gorgeous young mother's hand.

"I told a lie," Will said. He began to sob too hard to speak. I got the impression that was the idea. His mother apparently thought the same. "William," she said. "William?"

"I did pay Wayne," he sobbed, "just like he said. I got the $10 out of my mom's purse."

"But next time he won't have to," she declared. "Next time I'll give him $20 if that's how much it costs to stop that little sociopathic monster victimising my son every day."

"What did you call my boy, bitch?" Karl's dad stood up to demand.

She didn't blink. Will held onto her for dear life, but she didn't flinch. "A little sociopathic monster," she repeated evenly, "asshole."

I got home from all that to find a message on our answering machine from the police. They'd taken Al into custody after the driver of the 33 bus he was riding toward Dedham phoned to report that he was threatening her passengers. How much stress can anybody endure in a single afternoon? I felt as though I'd been up for 96 hours without sleep.

I got over to the station and paid his bail – $275 that I couldn't afford. We went out to my car. He chewed frantically, though there was nothing in his mouth.

He admitted he hadn't taken his medication in five days. As far as he was concerned, he wanted to get off it for good. He couldn't blame me, given how bloated he'd come to look, for not wanting to fuck him. Not, of course, that he'd be able to do it properly anyway. If he had to choose between having to contend with the occasional voice in his head and being constantly constipated, and looking as though he'd been inflated with a bicycle pump and wanting to sleep all the time, but never being able to, at least not very soundly, he'd take the occasional voice.

Like the one he'd heard on the bus, which had told him to determine which Frank Black albums his fellow passengers liked best, and then to try to make those who said anything other than *The Orange Album* see how foolish they were being. Everyone's "pretending" that he or she didn't even have a Frank Black album had made him angry. He'd sat down in disgust, but the voice he was hearing called him a wuss for it, so he'd challenged a couple of passengers, demanding to know why they were lying. When a pair of teenagers called him a head case, he hadn't actually touched them, but only said he was going to find out where they lived and cut their parents' hearts out with his Swiss Army knife-like multifunction tool, which in fact he'd forgotten at home.

Didn't his not having actually laid a finger on them demonstrate that he could do fine without the fucking risperidone? Well, didn't it?

20

The Bells of Success

"WHAT really rubs me the wrong way," Charles was heard to grouse, "is English critics dumping on me for incorporating a country or Southern rock influence. 'It's not his right.' Well, I've been around country music and folk music my whole fucking life. How *dare* someone say it would not be authentic to incorporate that stuff into my own music?"

The big problem – the problem that wouldn't die – was that Charles was forever having to compete with himself, around this time, it was with 4AD's compilation *The Absolute Bottom Of The Barrel*, or *The Pixies: Complete B Sides*, or whatever they called it. Moreover, Smirnoff had licensed the use of 'Tame' for adverts for its vodka. And 'Where Is My Mind' could be heard in the popular Brad Pitt vehicle *Fight Club*.

"When you don't get played on the radio," Charles sighed in relation to the Smirnoff deal, "you start to not be as picky about opportunities to have your music heard or to have your name in print. So, you know, if some beer company calls and says, 'Hey, we want to use your song in a beer ad,' when I was younger, I might have had some kind of high and mighty idea that that isn't cool. But when you get older, you're just like, 'Screw this, whatever you're selling, I don't give a shit.' The same people that own the radio stations own the liquor companies. It's all connected."

"When you used to be associated with something that was financially more successful, and also critically acclaimed," he told another writer, seemingly with notable candour, "I think it's hard to get away from that until you once again ring the bells of success. People are always going to say, 'Yeah, great record – but not quite as good as that old *Doolittle* record.' I'm not sure why. I'm just guessing it has to do with the bottom line. Maybe I'm wrong. Maybe my records now just aren't as good."

"It felt like a solid plateau with a good view," Charles would later say of *Dog*, speaking less plainly than usual. "As opposed to *Pistolero* before it, which was an interesting, rocky place to be. To make really great records is not about the great song that you wrote, it's about all the other songs you have to go through to get to that really great moment."

He made no attempt to conceal his glee about the album having been recorded, for around $50,000 all in, in the same way the classic records of yesteryear had been, "live to two-track [although in the old days, of course, it had been live to mono], no edits or splices. It isn't that peculiar for the older guys in bands to have come up that way, but I never did – I started multi-tracking, punching in and the like. Now, I go for the faster and cheaper and more live-sounding thing." When he mused, "I foresee a time when we will record to wax cylinder, or perhaps release only on sheet music," *Gigantic* was duly amused.

"You don't necessarily get speed out of it," he said of recording direct to stereo. "You *can* get speed out of it, but you can also get just as bogged down as with multi-track recording. What are the advantages? Well, it's real. It's a recording of a real performance, as opposed to a facsimile of that, which is frequently what people do with multi-track recording. It's got a little more heart."

We won't argue the part about heart, but the facsimile part begs to be addressed again. When little Peter or Pauline Punter slips a CD into his or her player in his or her bedroom on the outskirts of Andover, what he or she hears is indeed a facsimile of a performance, either a fussed-over, idealised facsimile, if a lot of overdubbing and digital editing and so on took place, or a more true-to-life facsimile. But the only way to provide a non-facsimile would be for the band actually to perform right there in the bedroom, and there isn't nearly enough room, Charles alone requiring substantial cubic footage.

By June, they were ready to hit the road anew, even though it was scheduled to take them this time to the Cat's Cradle in Carrboro, North Carolina, a town of which not even Americans have heard. One must make his own fun in a place like Sioux Falls, and Charles amused himself by coming up with the idea of playing 'Six Sixty-Six' as though it were a Black Sabbath or Sonic Youth song, rather than a Larry Norman, at a fraction of the tempo of the recorded version. The band also worked Arlo Guthrie's 'Coming Into Los Angeles', Bryan Ferry's 'Remake/Remodel', and Elvis' career low point 'Song Of The Shrimp' (from the *Girls! Girls! Girls!* soundtrack) into their repertoire. They became accustomed, in the opening bars of 'Where Is My Mind?' to their audiences happily providing the *whoo-ooh*.

When Jean got ill late in June, Charles flew home from Texas and a dozen remaining gigs were cancelled. By late autumn, she was back in the pink, and Charles flew to good old reliable Europe for seven solo performances in Hamburg (one of them for journalists), Paris, and London.

He returned for a series of shows in California with Dave Philips on lead guitar. At the Knitting Factory, where his opening act was the self-described scientific experimentalist David Lovering, he was joined by none other than Joseph A. Santiago, now with rather more forehead than in the days when *People* named him the Sexiest Man Alive. During his act, David Lovering, who, after playing with Cracker and working with Nitzer Ebb on an album that wound up not getting finished, had had his drums cryogenically frozen, made lightbulbs explode in his hands, illuminated a fluorescent tube held by a volunteer, and induced various objects to crackle and spark, all as though by magic!

Very much more garrulous than when on a bigger stage, Charles introduced his first number as being about Samson and Delilah, delighting the Pixies fan present who recalled the references in 'Gouge Away' to being chained to the pillars. Philips did a nice job evoking Joey's original lead guitar, and Charles howled exultantly. But it was while performing six songs from *Dog* (and four additional new tunes that would be used for B-sides), that the two guitarists really hit their stride. Delighted with the audience's delight, Charles slipped into his raconteur mode between songs and even played a bit of 'Monkey Gone To Heaven'.

"My wife," he told an interviewer who'd asked about his latest work, "said, 'Gee, you're really writing a lot of great songs, Charles, but everyone's gonna think I'm a bitch.' But sometimes you just write songs. Some of them are from your own personal experience, but they're not from my diary this month, not this-is-what-I-did-on-my-summer-vacation. A lot of times they're just things that happened to you a long time ago, or to people in your family."

And whether they were confessional or purest fiction, he was still, after all these years, having the same old trouble. "Composing lyrics," Charles would later confess, "is fun and easy to do – once I get going. Until I actually break the ice, it's like some algebra homework assignment hanging over my head. 'Aw, shit, I still haven't done my homework. Oh, man, I'm gonna get in trouble.' It's like this chore.

"I always forget how much I enjoy it. Then when I actually sit down and do it, it's like, 'Oh yeah, I love doing this!' You'd think I would learn after so many years. I should just do it. For some reason it just isn't like that for me, as opposed to picking up a guitar, which is way easier, I guess because it's less intellectual."

He might not have been very good anymore (if, indeed, he ever was) but he was certainly prolific, as here, simultaneously came not just one new album barely a year after the woeful *Dog*, but two, *Devil's Workshop* and *Black Letter Days*, released simultaneously. Why, he was asked, not a double album? "Well, it's two different sections, two different line-ups, two different producers. So it's sort of out of deference to some of the people involved. I didn't mix and match, I just kind of left them separate."

"I try my best not to give them every little piece of drivel that goes through my mind," Frank had long since assured another interviewer by this time, but there are plenty of moments on these two albums that strongly suggest otherwise – along with some of the most interesting stuff in the Frank Black canon. *Gigantic*'s own favourites are in *BLD*'s rootsy mid-section. In 'End Of Miles', in which he memorably describes himself as feeling "leathery and bleached", he manages an unprecedentedly successful visit to his usually ill-advised lower register, and sounds an authentic good old boy. A big instrumental rave-up celebrates his achievement. He also offers a convincing country blues-inflected vocal in '1826', which features an unusual guitar riff in 7/8. The bluesy 'The Farewell Bend' wryly has the singer demanding of his possibly straying lover, "Where are you going and honey, who did you befriend?" What a very genteel way of putting it!

He sings in a very peculiar voice indeed – it reminds one of Frank Zappa's mockeries of doo-wop lead singers – on 'Southbound Bevy', and spectacularly badly on the morose 'How You Went So Far', but manages to sound pretty heartfelt on both 'Jane The Queen Of Love', which is pretty easily heard as being addressed to Jean, his own queen, and the brooding 'Cold Heart Of Stone', on which he urges the person to whom he's singing, "If ever you need, don't call" – a nice twist on the usual idea of the jilted lover being eager to put his own pain and humiliation aside if the one who's caused them should ever need him.

He sings the title line of 'I Will Run After You' like a college student recording the first song he's ever made up into a cassette recorder. Boy, does this one plead for deliberate, more detailed production! As too does 'Valentine And Garuda', whose lyrics call out plaintively – and, of course, in vain – for sonic evocations of Eastern Europe. There are those who believe this track to contain Frank's first recorded guitar solo. It's far less shambolic than Bob Dylan's on 'Leopard Skin Pillbox Hat', and consequently less endearing.

"I think we pursue hi-fi as much as we ever did," Charles had recently said, "and, if anything, more so, because I want to prove to everybody that it's a good thing." With the startlingly lo-fi *Black Letter Days*, he seemed farther than ever from realising that ambition.

"He's . . . got more than a bit of Thomas Pynchon in him . . .," Scott Thill observed for *Pop Matters*. "His songs are so jam-packed with cultural allusion and interrogation that you need a lyrical companion to make sense of it all." Well, you're not going to make much sense of it *with* a lyric sheet, but you're better off with it than with the actual artist's explanation of 'True Blue', for instance: "There's this repeated phrase 'In a little while'. What happens is, in the following line, after 'In a little while', the last syllable always is a syllable from that phrase, 'in a little while'. For example, 'in a little while', the following is 'I'm gonna do some wanderin''. 'In a little while' the next one is 'so let's pass the narghile'. Then the second half it does the same thing, and it may do it in reverse.

"The music is in reverse too. There's the 'A' section, then the 'B' section. It goes back to the 'A' section, but then the 'C' section is really the 'B' section played backwards. There's this whole theme in the lyric, what it's all about, and there's a whole frontward and backward kind of thing there.

"There's one – this is all theoretical – strain of humanity which devolves, if you want to call it that, and returns to the sea, from whence we came. Maybe tens of thousands of years from now, people will hang out more by the seaside and gradually begin this march back to the ocean. The singer of the song is of that strain in the second half, but in the first half the singer is that strain of humanity that moves away, not only from where we are on the land, but away from planet Earth. They go up – up and out as opposed to the other direction. It's all tied in with the frontwards backwards of the lyrics. It's just this incredibly overcomplicated neurotic kind of thing."

All this for a musically unremarkable song lasting less than two minutes, and too long at that.

"That's just some little ditty on the record, but sometimes that's what you do when you write a ditty. You become consumed by some little game you're playing. It's almost like it's not in your own control."

The only interesting aspect of both 'Heloise' and 'The Kingly Cave' is the lyrics, and without knowing that the latter was inspired by the infamous 12th century nun whose affair with a theology professor ended in his castration (it's always the intellectual who gets punished, innit?) and the other by Charles' visit to Graceland, they'd only be baffling. The latter song, Charles told an interviewer, was "about a trip I took to Graceland many years ago. I thought it would be fun to take hallucinogenic mushrooms while I was there. It's not something I would really do now. I was young and dumb and I went to Graceland with my girlfriend and we took mushrooms and it was a horrible tense day."

As to why *Black Letter Days* both began and ended with Tom Waits' 'The Black Rider', he revealed, "We started to play that at our show about a year and a half ago. We tried a couple of different covers when we were recording, but that was the one that we did the best. Even then, I wasn't happy with the way we were doing it . . . so we started to fool around with it a bit and have some fun, and the result was one reel of tape with probably seven different versions, one devolving into the next and getting sillier. What you hear are the first take and last take. There was a lyrical omission in the first, preferred version. I was frustrated that the preferred take had this lyric missing because of my mistake. Everyone liked this other, sillier version as well."

Gigantic, no curmudgeon, will not mention that if they hadn't painted themselves into a corner by recording direct to stereo, rectifying the omission would have been easy-peasy.

Noting the darkness of the nominal themes on *Devil's Workshop* – 'The Kingly Cave' is about mortality, 'Bartholomew' about insanity, and 'Whiskey In Your Shoes' about losing a child – a writer asked if Charles felt himself becoming more serious. "I don't know," Charles mused. "I think I'm probably more comfortable now singing songs that are not abstract or so surreal. I think I'm a lot more comfortable writing songs that have a meaning or a narrative."

If only!

Did no one think to mention to Charles that 'Out Of State' is extremely in the wrong key for him? Behold the juxtaposition of a big end-of-the-world metal guitar and the weediest snare drum sound in the history of recorded music on 'Fields Of Marigold' – this makes poor Gary Smith's sound in comparison like the famous gated reverb sound Hugh Padgham worked up for Phil Collins. One has to admire the huge slide guitar sound on 'Whiskey In Your Shoes', but to shudder at the muddy distortion that clutters 'Are You Headed My Way', among other tracks.

So it's an unedited live performance. So bloody what? And this too must be asked: in a world in which there are Jeff Beck and Steve Vai and Eddie Van Halen and Jan Cyrka and Joe Satriani and Richard Thompson, how does a guitarist like Dave Philips muster the gall to play solo after solo? He's certainly a competent musician, but haven't we heard it all a thousand times before, better? Does he ever startle you, ever make you laugh, ever once break your heart? Not to be belabour the point, but where's Charles' old antipathy to guitar solos now that he needs it most?

21

(Vicky's Story)
An Interest, Not An Obsession

MAYBE there was something in the water. Or maybe it wasn't the water I drank at home, but at the hospital when I visited Al there after Dr. Pompous, his smug jargon-spewing psychiatrist, committed him. Not that I condemned the decision. I couldn't devote my life to caring for him, to ensuring that he took his medication, and if he didn't, he was unmistakably, in the classic sense, a danger both to himself and to others.

Seeing him in the hospital was heartbreaking. He was up to 200 pounds (having weighed something like 135 in the Do What Thou Wilt days) now – 200 heavy, lethargic pounds. The half-dozen gaudiest streetwalkers in southern New England could have strutted past him without his noticing. When I tried to talk to him, his glazed eyes would focus on me only intermittently. He sucked implacably, like one dying of thirst trying to get the last drop of juice out of a carton he'd found in the bottom of his lifeboat.

Lifeboat. God, didn't all that – the Rat and Gary Smith and sharing the little apartment in Cambridge with Her Perf – seem around a million years ago?

But I was getting used to heartbreak. While Al was being committed, Nanci was busy dying of lung cancer in her and her not-so-ridiculous (in fact, pretty nearly saintly) boyfriend Derek's cruddy studio apartment down in Quincy, attended by the ever-faithful Derek and a hospice volunteer, so full of morphine that she wouldn't have been able to tell when she left this world and entered the next.

She hadn't taken no for an answer after that horrible afternoon when I met her at the coffee shop in Eastie. She'd not only become a loyal friend to me and Tricia, but had devoted herself – apparently with Derek's blessing – to saving my dad. And she'd managed it somehow. When she gave him the $1,800 dollars she'd saved for Tricia, it was with the understanding that he use however much of it he had to get himself rehabilitated.

He spent nine days drying out at this place up in Maine, the Arbors. I contributed $300. When he got home, Nanci and Tricia and I took turns taking him to AA meetings. He went to five a week, of which Nanci took him to three. She spent endless hours on the bus, but never faltered. Tricia credits her with having saved her marriage, with helping her and Dennis come to understand how they were hurting each other as the marriage therapist they consulted hadn't even begun to do.

Life is so full of cruel ironies of different sizes and shapes. Alan, who fervently loathed the expression "it sucks", now spent his days sucking frantically, without realising. And Nanci, who'd been smoking from age 14, and then finally managed, on what she estimated was her 25th attempt, to beat it at 52, died of lung cancer six years later.

In her last weeks, she looked about as awful as I imagine it possible for a human being to look, and knew it. She asked Tricia, who's taken some photography classes at night school, and shot some really gorgeous photos of her and Den's daughters – photos I'm convinced she ought to enter in competitions – to take some pictures, which she asked us to put unretouched online and send to all the tobacco companies. She also wondered if *Maxim* might be interested in a couple of the sultrier ones. Her sense of humour stayed intact until the morphine dulled it.

But back to what was or wasn't in the water, and to the unmistakable signs that I was beginning to lose it myself. Once a week, my third graders get an hour's instruction in what the school district calls Music Appreciation from this very sweet young woman a few months out of college named Louisa, whose real interest is apparently in singing opera. One week she'll pass out recorders and try to teach the kids a very simple tune (God, what an unholy din!). The next, she'll get them to listen to a current hit record that they've probably heard an older sibling or even parent play, and try to help them recognise and articulate what they like or don't like about it.

The kids enjoy these sessions a lot more than I do. On recorder days, I have to be very vigilant to make sure Karl doesn't bash someone over the head with his.

The last time Louisa was in, I suggested that, instead of the Beyoncé single she'd had in mind, she talk to the kids about Frank Black. I pointed out that he'd been making really interesting, unusual music for 14 years, whereas Beyoncé would be lucky to be remembered in three. She'd never heard of Frank Black, but was pretty sure she'd heard of the Pixies. "Weren't they on that cute cartoon show on PBS a couple of years ago?" she asked. The poor benighted thing. As it happened, I had *Trompe Le Monde* in my CD Walkman, and lent it to her.

I asked her the next week in the teachers' lounge what she'd thought of it. "Well," she said, looking as though she wished herself elsewhere, "it was a little bit . . . *out there* for my own taste, with that screaming and everything. I actually found it sort of scary."

I said kids loved scary things, and felt strongly that we needed to talk about the album with my class.

A part of that was familiar – very much the sort of dry, provocative humour in which I've always specialised, the kind that involves teasing someone very covertly at first, and then more and more overtly until they get the joke, *if* they get it. But a part of it was new and a little scary. I wasn't at all sure this time that *I* got the joke, or even if there was a joke involved. Louisa studied my face for clues that I was teasing her, but found none, and I was alarmed to realise I wasn't so sure myself.

She said she wasn't sure the Pixies were appropriate for third grade music appreciation, but I wouldn't – *couldn't* – take no for an answer. "Do you really want to create a new generation of fucking Beyoncé fans," I heard myself demand, "or actually expand their tastes for once?"

The second the word passed my lips I knew something was wrong. Louisa's face hardened. She thought maybe we'd better consult Mr. Coleman.

We consulted him. He asked Louisa if he and I could have a moment. He touched my shoulder and told me he understood how difficult it must be for me, as he'd had an uncle who'd had to be institutionalised for depression. But surely I could understand that Louisa, as the district's music teacher, was entitled to autonomy in terms of determining her curriculum. Surely I appreciated too that obscene language was entirely inappropriate at school. "Autonomy," I repeated contemptuously, "curriculum. It's just jargon, just educationspeak. What I'm talking about is opening these young people up to a fantastic new experience."

He didn't know quite what to say. But I was just getting started. "Do you know their work?" I demanded. "Do you know that this group essentially invented a new form of rock'n'roll? Do you appreciate how difficult that is, how rare? They say there's nothing new under the sun, but the Pixies refuted that. And this is a group that started out right here in Boston. Can you imagine the pride these children will feel when they learn that?"

He was just gaping at me, and I realised with that I'd been shouting. But how could they all be so fucking . . . what was that word? . . . obdurate?

"I think you'd better take the rest of the week off, Vicky," he said. "It's my impression that the real and very understandable stress you've been under is really beginning to take its . . ."

"And the Pixies were only the first chapter of Charles Thompson's career. Are you aware that he's actually recorded more music as a solo artist than as a member of the Pixies? Now, I'm not saying his solo stuff has been consistently brilliant in the same way the Pixies were, because it hasn't been – there were moments on *Teenager* and *Ray* well below his usual standard. I'm not going to debate that with you. What I am going to assert is that this is a true American original, if you will, whose work richly – *richly* – deserves to be studied in the schools."

Talk about irony. Mr. Coleman had got the school maintenance man, Hiroshi, to rig up a panic button after the scary meeting at which Karl's dad intimidated everybody. By pressing it, unbeknownst to me, he'd summoned our campus security guard, a 66-year-old former Boston cop named Ray. And here Ray was, tapping on Mr. Coleman's door and then letting himself in, breathless from having run over.

I couldn't believe it. Well, if Mr. Coleman wanted to be a dick, maybe Ray, the salt of the earth, would be more open-minded. "Do *you* know the Pixies' work, Ray?" I asked him. "I mean, I recognise you're probably a little older than most of their audience, and that you're probably more of a Sinatra man, or Tony Bennett, or one of those guys, right? And please understand I'm not for a minute saying those guys are corny old *schtick*mongers who haven't actually contributed the slightest . . ."

"Come along, Ms. Tighe," Ray said gently. "Here we go now." He actually had his hand on me. I was actually being forcibly evicted!

Ray stayed with me until I got on my bus. I burst into tears as it pulled away from the kerb and didn't stop crying until we were a block from my house. Once inside, I immediately got online, and had live chats with other fans in the *frankblack.net* forum chatroom. There's always a Frank Black fanatic awake and eager to chat somewhere in the world. When I lost my connection and saw what time it was, I realised I had a problem. I'd been at it 12 hours.

I saw a shrink — not the jargon-spewing one who'd committed Al, not Dr. Pompous, but a really nice one who didn't use any jargon at all, a woman I could easily picture having been pretty ravishing in her day. I told her how I was finding it increasingly difficult to think about anything other than Frank Black and the Pixies. Everything else seemed terribly uninteresting in comparison. She asked if I had any sexual fantasies involving Frank, and I admitted that I did, even though I knew him to be both married and faithful. I told her about Al, and said I was very resistant to the idea of treating whatever problem I might be said to have pharmacologically.

She asked if I didn't regard having been suspended from my job as a problem. I told her I thought it was the school district's problem, not being able to accommodate the passions of its teachers. "I mean, isn't passionate teaching exactly the kind we want most? Do we really want our children taught by listless lifers dragging themselves to retirement age, toeing the line every step of the way?"

I thought I'd put that pretty compellingly, but Dr. Flanagan just made a little notation in her notebook instead of responding. She really wanted me to consider a low dosage of a medication she'd found to be helpful in cases very much like my own. In the meantime, she encouraged me to join a therapy group that, as luck would have it, was having its second meeting that night.

The group, led by Sol, a sweet-natured Ph.D. candidate with thick globular clumps of curly black hair on either side of his head, and a huge, shiny, bald expanse on top, turned out to have members as young as 19 and as old as 62. At the beginning, each of us had to say their name, how old they were, and with whom they were obsessed. The 19-year-old, Danny, was obsessed – non-sexually, we were to understand – with Fred Durst, the lead singer of the heavy metal/hip-hop hybrid Limp Bizkit, 62-year-old Leonard with Tina Turner. There were two Jennifer Aniston obsessives, one of each sex, both in their early thirties. There was a 51-year-old academic-looking guy (his corduroy sports coat even had fake leather patches on the elbows) who played implacably with the pipe he wasn't allowed to smoke inside, and worried that his fascination with Britney Spears was ruining his life.

When I told them I was Vicky, aged 29, but refused to characterise my interest in Frank Black as an obsession, the butch lesbian Jennifer Aniston fan said, "Yeah, right," in disgust. "Not an obsession, just an 'interest'."

"Remember, Caitlin," Sol said, "we don't make judgments here. We just try to hear one another."

Caitlin and the other Jennifer Aniston obsessive, a small, high-strung guy in thick glasses, a guy you could easily have pictured doing people's taxes for a living, wasted no time getting in a little shouting match about their respective achievements the past week. The accountant had persuaded four people in the building his office was in to join Jennifer's official fan club, even though it cost money. Caitlin had received a letter from Jennifer's lawyer advising her to stop writing letters to Jennifer.

"I actually *did* something for Jennifer," the little guy said contemptuously. "What you did only caused her to worry. And you call yourself a Jennifer person!"

"Abe," Sol said to the 62-year-old, who seemed to spend most of his time under a sun lamp, and who I think was wearing a toupee, though I seem never to have been as good at spotting them as most people, "we didn't really get a chance last week to hear your story." Definitely wearing no socks under his white patent loafers, Abe smiled brightly – you could picture him having his teeth bleached a couple of times a year – and made himself slightly more comfortable, as though he were a guest on a talk show just asked a question he was going to enjoy answering. He told us how he had seen the Ike & Tina Turner Revue while studying for his MBA. "I'd never been so aroused by an entertainer in my life, and never would be again, although the opening sequence of *Lenny*, with Valerie Perrine as Lenny Bruce's stripper wife, came pretty close."

"Keep on task, please, Abe," Sol said.

"Sorry. I mean, she was something else, the way she whipped her hair around, the way she strutted around on those very high heels, the way she snarled. It was all so . . . primal. It just made my pecker go *boing!*"

"Jesus, spare us the gory details, will you?" Caitlin, who apparently didn't relish accounts of heterosexuality, complained. But Abe just ignored her.

"I saw 14 shows on her farewell tour," he said, seemingly expecting the rest of us to contort with envy. "Fourteen. And thoroughly enjoyed every minute of every last one of them."

"But what about the bad parts, Abe?" Sol asked gently. "What about the disruptive parts?"

"There haven't been any, at least for me. I mean, sure, my wife left me. But who's to say she wouldn't have left me six months down the line for some other reason, you know? As far as work, hey, I'm retired. I can devote myself to Tina to my heart's content.

"And I do. And I thoroughly enjoy every second of it. I have one of the three largest collections of photographs of Tina in concert in the world, and I'm adding to it every day. Thank God for eBay!"

Considering how happy he seemed with his life, I don't know why I found him really creepy, but I did, and I'd have bet the others did too.

Sol asked if I'd like to tell everyone about myself in greater detail. I wasn't feeling very comfortable with everybody yet, and revealed only that I'd come to regard Frank Black, formerly Black Francis of the Pixies, as the most important popular musician of the 21st century.

"You couldn't say that if Tina weren't retired," Abe said, no longer beaming. "I wouldn't allow it. Unless of course by musician you mean somebody who plays an instrument. I suppose I'd call Tina more of an entertainer than a musician." He turned to the young Limp Bizkit fan, Danny, and asked, "How about you?"

"Just fuck off, will you, please?" Danny said. He turned to me. "The Pixies rocked. All that screaming and shit? Awesome. I think he might have inspired Fred."

I thought I'd leave it at that. These people were clearly nuts.

After a silence long enough to get everyone fidgeting, the academic-looking guy said, very solemnly, "I don't remember if I talked about this last week, but I think my obsession with Britney is a natural outgrowth of the celebrity culture engendered by capitalism. I honestly don't hold myself responsible."

"Yeah, you did tell us," Caitlin said. "It was boring as shit last week, and it'll be boring as shit again this week."

"Remember, Caitlin," Sol said, "hearing, not judging."

"My own opinion," Abe offered, "is that on the best day of her life little Ms. Spears won't be a thousandth the entertainer Tina was on the worst day of hers."

"Oh, fuck off with that Tina shit all the time," Danny Limp Bizkit said. "Fucking old lady. Fucking grandma."

"I could teach Britney things she isn't even aware she doesn't know," Caitlin said dreamily. "Her and the little slutty one, Aguilera."

"Fred nailed Britney, you know," Danny told her proudly. "And then dumped her. Served the bitch right."

Sol sighed deeply. I don't think things were going quite as he'd expected. So he took over. "I'm one of you," he announced. Everyone seemed to find that interesting enough to stop glaring at each other. "You can't really tell me anything about celebrity obsession I haven't experienced myself, from the inside. For 18 months, I couldn't really think about anything or anybody but Keanu Reeves. I sent him something like 4,200 emails, and nearly a thousand snail mail letters and postcards. My walls were floor-to-ceiling with his likeness. I spent a fortune buying amateur recordings of his band Dogstar on eBay. I set two places at dinner each night, imagining that one night he'd actually show up. It was folly, but such pleasurable folly. I won't deny that there are parts of it I miss.

"Yes, I'm gay. That's something I was able to come to terms with only through my obsession with Keanu, by the way."

"Are we talking about the dark young chap from *The Matrix*," Abe asked. "Oh, my, he's perfectly dreadful, though. Couldn't act his way out of a wet paper bag, I don't think."

"Me and my girlfriend rented *The Devil's Advocate* on DVD a couple of months ago," the little male Jennifer Aniston fan related, brightening through his thick glasses at the thought. "We couldn't believe our eyes. Could the guy be any more wooden? How did Pacino keep from bursting out laughing when they were playing opposite each other?"

"I'll take him over fucking Ben Stiller," Danny contributed darkly. "Dude's got zero charisma – like none. At least Keanu looks good. Ben Stiller's like the little dweebs whose lunch money I used to steal every morning before school."

Sol smiled with satisfaction. "What I want you all to notice is that sometimes it's nearly impossible to imagine what someone else sees in the celebrity we're personally obsessed with. I think recognising that in many cases is the first step toward recovering from the obsession. But now let's take 15 minutes to use the little boys' and girls' rooms."

22

He Is Not a Dancing Bear

A COMMON misconception is that Charles wasn't much interested in music until Joey Santiago introduced him to that of Iggy Pop in their U-Mass dormitory suite. But that he'd been writing songs inspired by Velvet Underground from age 15 came out in his confessions about *Workshop*'s 'Velvety', which, as 'Velvety Instrumental Version', had been a Pixies B-side years before. "We had started to play it when we were touring on *Dog In The Sand*, just as an instrumental – a loud 'Hello! We're here!' kind of rave-up. One day when I had a session, but didn't have a new song to present to the band, I said, 'OK, I'm gonna write some lyrics to this song.' As a matter of fact, that was the first thing we recorded for *Devil's Workshop.*

"I had called it 'Velvety Instrumental Version' because at the time I thought it sounded like The Velvet Underground, which, of course, it doesn't, in hindsight. So then I was kind of stuck with that – now I've got to write the lyricised version of 'Velvety'. So I had to think about what 'Velvety' meant to me. It's really lyrically the sister song of 'Velouria', the same character, the same imagery, part of the same Northern California, and Mount Shasta lore. I may have incorporated a line or two from the original lyrics from when I was 15.

"I was like, 'So now I have to write a song about some woman named Velvety.' That became the lyrical direction of the song. I like those kinds of random parameters. That's what songs are a lot of the time – just games you play. Sometimes it's a language thing. Sometimes it's a meter thing, or a rhyming thing. There are all kinds of neurotic little games going on."

The neurotic little games he played with his own lyrics became almost as popular a topic with interviewers as direct-to-stereo. "Even if you write about nothing," he told one of them, "even if you write a bunch of abstract poetry, you've got to come up with *something*. Half the time I don't know what the songs are about, because I'm so consumed by some weird little abstract game in my mind. Five years later, 'Hey, what's "Los Angeles" about?' Man, I don't remember. I was having some crazy thought."

OK, Mr. Modern Rock God, herewith some new not-so-random parameters you might enjoy. Write some coherent songs that speak, in a reasonably comprehensible way, of the particular pains and pleasures of being Charles Michael Kittridge Thompson IV. Is 'The Last Stand Of Shazeb Andleeb' about xenophobia, and maybe even a fatal expression thereof? If so, how do you feel about it, or, at the very least, describe what you observed and let us make up our own minds. Lose five points for every hifalutin red herring (*thalossocracy*, say, or *choragic*) you toss in. Lose 10 points for every instance of letting rhyme or meter compel nonsensicality. And receive 1,000 points for every song that makes a non-pre-sold listener (we acknowledge that your preternaturally devoted fans find your every last bit of, well, drivel inexpressibly glorious) feel a little less alone in the universe because of your vivid evocation of something he or she too has felt. Write your own 'For No One'.

Fat (no pun intended) chance.

He contributed a track to *Wig In A Box*, an album of reconsiderations of songs from *Hedwig And The Angry Inch*, the off-Broadway rock musical-turned-film about an East German transsexual rocker with an incompetent surgeon, benefiting a New York organisation dedicated to serving "lesbian, gay, bisexual, transgender and questioning youth". Along with David Byrne and others less notable, he also did a track for a former-Devo-members-produced album of music inspired by the Cartoon Network series *The Powerpuff Girls*, a rather less altruistic undertaking.

In the meantime, the former Mrs. John Murphy maintained a home on Nantucket, but actually lived most of the time in the East LA barrio, where she drank her share of tequila, played ballads on the jukebox, alternately laughed maniacally at or got hostile around interviewers, and had nothing bad to say about Charles.

"I'm not one of those people that's real attached to where I live," she explained. "I don't really care about anything but smoking pot and playing music, and it doesn't matter where I am as long as I can do that."

A couple of weeks into 2001, he about whom Kim had nothing bad to say began a tour of the Eastern edge of his and The Catholics' home continent in front of three of The Catholics' hometown fans, at the Met Café in Providence. They made it again to Winooski, Vermont, and Carrboro, North Carolina, and then, after an appearance at Manhattan's Mercury Lounge, back over to the UK, their second night in which they performed at King Tut's Wah Wah Hut in Glasgow, and lived to tell the tale. After delighting their audience at the Astoria in London by including the Pixies' 'Dancing The Manta Ray', 'Gouge Away', 'Monkey Gone To Heaven', and 'Where Is My Mind', they headed for continental Europe, this time finding four places to play in Holland, a country that could fit in Rhode Island's hip pocket with room for most of Luxembourg.

While there, Charles did a remarkably candid and revealing interview with *OOR*, talking about everything from the effect of the endless uprootings of his boyhood to his divorce. He'd come to realise in psychotherapy, he said, that the flipside of the fierce independence he'd cultivated as a child, when he could never be sure he'd have the same friends for longer than a few months, was the difficulty he had bonding with people. Hadn't Joe suggested something very similar in explaining why he hadn't even tried to get Charles to talk about breaking up the Pixies?

He spoke of 'Massif Centrale' as being about his very genuine desire to "snuggle under a rock and shelter until the worst pain disappeared". He spoke of the pain of not having anywhere to come home to after his and Jean's separation – "Having a home is elementary for me" – and revealed that it was his and Jean's irreconcilable feelings about children (she didn't share his desire for them) that had made their parting inevitable, though they continued to love one another. He even recommended psychotherapy for everyone.

"My wife," he admitted to another questioning youth around the same time, "had been trying to get me to go down this road of being a little more direct for some years. So I had to go find something to make me cry, some artificial thing. 'Why don't you get a sad movie,' [my therapist] said. 'Are you kidding me? I laugh at people that cry at films.' Having said that, I got into this Elliott Smith record I discovered through *The Royal Tenenbaums*. I can pop on 'Needle In The Hay', and in 30 seconds I'll be bawling like a baby."

What was most striking about the personality he exhibited on the stage of the Shepherd's Bush Empire the night *Gigantic* saw him perform there with The Catholics was how very little pleasure he seemed to derive from the pleasure of his audience, whom he simply ignored. He'd earlier petulantly defended his aloofness in the course of responding to questions of his preternaturally devoted fans on the FrankBlack.net website: "I write songs. I record them. I go on tour and I play them. That's all. I don't ask people to 'put their hands together' or any other show biz crap . . . I am a guitar player. I am not a dancing bear. I am a singer. I am not a dancing bear. I am a guy loading a trailer [to save money, The Catholics no longer employed roadies]. I am not a dancing bear.

"Sometimes people think I'm rude when I don't switch into that dancing bear routine. I am not complaining. I adore playing music to the people that support my art. But I am not a fucking dancing bear."

While Charles was no dancing bear on stage, pencil-slim, grey-haired Rich Gilbert palpably relished the spotlight. His footwork was fancy. He played his guitar with a drumstick, or with his teeth, or so he made it appear, and, alone among The Catholics, seemed actually to have changed out of the clothes he'd worn all day in the van. For much of his first European tour, 'twas whispered, he'd been a vision in red (vinyl suit) and lime green (shoes).

After two weeks off, Charles and band were back in North America, which turned out to have a very rude welcome home up its sleeve. On the morning of April 13, they were horrified to discover that, since coming off the stage of Philadelphia's Trocadero the night before, someone had sneaked onto the car park of the Lester, Pennsylvania, EconoLodge and made off with the trailer containing their gear, specifically: two Fender Precision bass guitars (serial numbers 604578 and 329564), three Fender Telecaster guitars

(26673, 166209, 231549), a Gibson SG Jr. guitar (836489), a Sho-Bud pedal steel guitar (7655), a Guild guitar (FS-46EJ10010), a Gibson SG guitar (81664524), a Mullen pedal steel guitar (2421), a Fender Deluxe amplifier (200442), a Fender Twin Reverb amplifier (A07555), three Vox AC-30 amplifiers (13827, 12812b and M-19999-41-1600-B), a Bag End speaker cabinet (230027), a Trace Elliott amplifier (6130169), an SWR amplifier (2362725), an SWR Amplifier (2362725), an Alesis QS6 keyboard (S68003978), a Yamaha snare drum (SD455MO587), a Yamaha tom-tom (MTT-1116-LM-3723), another Yamaha tom-tom (MTT-1112-LM-3710), yet another Yamaha tom drum (MTT-1105-LM-3744), and another Yamaha snare drum (SD20756-ID-3955), not to mention a Godin guitar, a Gibson Les Paul Custom guitar, a Vox AC-30 cabinet, a Trace Elliot cabinet, five drum claws, four one-foot goosenecks, two Whirlwind Imp-2 microphones, two Sennheiser 409 microphones, nine Shure SM-57 microphones, ten Shure SM-58 microphones, a Shure SM-91 microphone, two AKG 451 microphones, an AKG D112 microphone, two Countryman direct boxes, a microphone case, a Zildjian cymbal set, assorted Yamaha drum hardware, 14 guitar tuners, 30 sets of guitar strings, 11 guitar bags, an Aphex compressor, a Sentrex power supply, 18 guitar pedals, two pedal steel guitar seats, nine guitar stands, various stage tools, various trailer tools, a partridge in a pear tree, and the trailer itself, all without serial numbers, but no less missed for it.

Bloody but unbowed (because insured), they cancelled their shows in Washington, DC and Pittsburgh, and re-equipped themselves in time to play three shows at Toronto's Horseshoe Tavern. The one the Toronto *Sun*'s gobsmacked reporter witnessed comprised 35 songs, and lasted a Springsteenian nearly three hours. In view of what had befallen them in Lester, Pennsylvania, it probably isn't coincidental that they slipped a version of Marvin Gaye's 'Can I Get A Witness?' into their show at Cleveland's Beachland Ballroom a few nights hence. Not even an upcoming performance at a venue in swinging Des Moines called Hairy Mary's could weaken their resolve. They got back to the West Coast for 15 dates and then took a couple of months off.

All other Breeders having sodded off over the years, the Deal twins now recruited guitarist Richard Presley, and the rhythm section of the East LA punk band Fear to play several live shows in 2001. The producers of *Buffy The Vampire Slayer* got wind of the fact that they were playing the show's theme song live at their gigs, and invited them to appear in the show, a substantial step up from getting a song onto the soundtrack of *The Mod Squad*. They reunited with Steve Albini to record the third Breeders studio album, 2002's *Title TK*, again on pre-digital equipment. The guitars were fuzzy, the sisters' harmonising even fuzzier, the tone rather darker, the performances wilfully ragged, the fi very lo. "The quaint attributes of this faux-relic," wrote Amazon.com's Kim Hughes, "quickly vanish as it becomes apparent there aren't a lot of ideas at work beneath the chilly atmospheric cooing and narcoleptic guitar strumming." It came to light that Kelley had resumed using, but had gone through rehab again, and had traded heroin for knitting, her speciality being handbags, which one could order from her own website.

Charles noted with particular disgust that KROQ, once the hippest station in the region of his birth, wouldn't actually play his music, but had no compunctions about appropriating instrumental bits of it for incidental use.

Having bought his own mobile recording set-up by now, he revealed that there were things about it he liked quite apart from its ability to allow him to make recordings with heart. "We move it around in a truck. It's not ready to go like a fire truck in two minutes – it takes us six hours to break it down. There's hydraulic lifts and things involved. I love being in a rock band, because it's just like being a kid. I just play with big blocks and trucks.

"We're gonna go and record again in a couple weeks because it's fun, not because we need to make another record. I mean, believe me, my record company's going to start pulling its hair out when I call them up in a month and say, 'Oh, by the way, we got this other record done and when can you release it?'"

The good news being that digitised recordings of Catholics shows were beginning to be downloaded in significant numbers now from furthurnet.com, a website popular with Grateful Dead obsessives, along with those of such beloved jam bands as Phish and Blues Traveler. Word had apparently got round that, given their huge (over 60 songs) repertoire and Rich Gilbert's playing different instruments as the whim struck him, no two shows were alike.

23

(Vicky's Story)
We Chuckfans

THERE was something I had to do before I left for the Coast, someone I had to see. And I'm not talking about Al, who'd made it very clear that he wanted nothing more to do with me so long as I remained an agent of al-Qaeda. It was nice to see the medication that had made him resemble an over-inflated balloon and destroyed his sex drive was doing such a good job of silencing the voices in his head.

Valina said sarcastically.

I loved him, and missed him, but how much can a person endure? I was about to turn 30, and wanted to do something more special than try to keep Karl from killing Will during the early part of the day, visiting Al in the late afternoon, and then having dinner with my dad and Tricia and Den and the girls. Not, of course, that I would have been trying to keep Karl from killing Will anyway, since I remained suspended with half-pay pending my psychiatric examination on the 16th.

I was taking carbamazepine and sertraline, and I had the phone numbers of all the others in Sol's celebrity obsessives group, as we were supposed to ask each other for moral support when we felt overwhelmed by the desire to contact our various celebrities. It sounded good in theory, but was another matter entirely in practice. Abe would phone to ask if I, whose field of expertise seemed to be pop music, knew any collectors who might have Tina Turner photos he hadn't seen – and if I might enjoy having cocktails with him some evening soon. (Cocktails! The word made me envision drinks with little umbrellas in them. With a 62-year-old man in a toupee!) And Danny the Limp Bizkit fan phoned to say he knew a guy who could get me Frank Black's home address for $300. I said no to the romantic evening with Abe and yes to Frank Black's home address. I couldn't really afford it, but how often does a person turn 30?

I called on Karl's dad at the motorcycle repair shop where he worked the afternoon before I flew out of Logan at 5.50 in the morning (because that was when Priceline could get me on a flight I could afford). He had to do all the cliché-embodying for the whole place, as one of the two other guys looked as much like a supermarket produce manager as a biker. The other, who couldn't have grown biker's muttonchop sideburns if he'd wanted to (he couldn't have been much older than 19) looked like a dropout from MIT.

I got exactly the warm welcome from Karl's dad I'd expected. He tore off the glasses I found it strangely endearing that he had to wear for work, strained to place me, and growled, "What's he did this time?"

What's he *did*. I sometimes wondered if these people stayed up past their bedtimes thinking of new ways to be ungrammatical.

"It isn't anything Karl done," I said. He didn't get the joke. "It's what you done."

Here came his sneer. "Yeah, and what's that?"

"Been a perfectly awful dad from the look of it," I said. "Being a complete fucking disaster as a parent."

"Bitch," he said, enjoying himself now. "Why don't you get your fat ass out of here before I . . ."

"Before you what? Before you demonstrate that you're physically stronger than a woman? Oh, that'll be impressive, won't it, guys?" I addressed myself to his two co-workers, but they pretended not to hear. "I've already seen a woman stare you down, you may recall, in Mr. Coleman's office."

He was considering crushing my trachea in one of his horrible hideous black hands. It was obvious. The fact that I didn't care – and God knows how I managed that – kept him from it.

"You're quite the badass with your seven-year-old son, aren't you? Seven years old and you've already damaged him so badly he might never recover. You must be really proud of yourself. Do the dudes you ride with admire you for that? Well, do they?"

He'd had his moment, during which brute indignation could have inspired him to hurt me physically. But another part of his abnormally small brain was calling the shots now, and I knew I was safe.

We glared at each other. If I had to stand there all day and miss my flight to LA, I wasn't going to blink first. "He's a good boy, my Karl," he finally said, looking away. "A little rambunctious, but a good kid deep down."

I kept glaring. His eyes came back to mine.

"Listen, my own childhood wasn't any fucking weekend at the beach, was it? If you think I'm not doing ten times better by Karl than my old man did by me, you're talking out of your ass, lady."

Lady, not bitch.

"You might be doing a thousand times better by him than your dad did by you," I said, "but that doesn't mean you're not fucking up big time. Whatever happened between you and your own dad should have nothing to do with Karl. Why should he have to suffer for stuff that went on years before he was even born? Why should any child?"

"Hey, guy," the MIT dropout with peach fuzz called, "we've got a lot of bikes we have to get out by end of day, remember."

Karl's dad actually winced. So the MIT dropout was his boss. I revelled in his embarrassment, smirking so he'd know it.

And then, on the way home to pack for my trip, I felt bad about what I'd done. When you came right down to it, my bullying his dad intellectually wasn't necessarily much more palatable than Karl bullying Will physically.

Yes: Valina. When I got back from California, I'd be 30 years old. At some point, given that Al seemed to be getting worse, and not better, I'd be starting a new relationship. If the school district's psychiatrist had it in for me, and I didn't get reinstated as a teacher, I'd have to find a new profession. I figured I deserved a new name too. Vicky was an awkward, self-loathing teenager's name. I decided to call myself after one of my favourite Pixies songs, 'Havalina', but then read somewhere that it meant wild boar in Spanish. So I short-ened it. I was used to my name starting with a V.

Charles' neighbourhood in the San Fernando Valley could hardly have been more blandly suburban. His street looked in the late after-noon haze like a set from a Steven Spielberg film – all huge front lawns and two-car garages, with groups of little girls riding by on bicycles with pink tyres and saddles and teenage boys either tossing a football back and forth or conferring about where to get the best price on crack. You could picture the air being full of the smell of barbecuing in the summer and intense boredom the other nine months.

Charles' house was in a cul-de-sac. It would somehow have felt weird just going and knocking on his door in broad daylight, and I was ravenous, so I went looking for a place to eat. I drove around for 20 minutes without seeing anything other than chain restaurants. It was hard to imagine how someone like Charles could choose to live in such a neck of the woods. No, it was impossible. I'd have figured him, if he had to live in LA, to live in one of the canyons, or in Silverlake, where I understood the likes of Beck (with whom Lyle Workman was now playing) hung their hats. I wound up settling for a bean burrito from Taco Bell.

The kids had gone inside by the time I got back to Charles' cul-de-sac. There were lots of cars (and not a few boats) in drive-ways, but only one other car on the actual street. The sun went down, and a feeling of the most unspeakable desolation came over the place. It was quarter past six on a Saturday afternoon, and it felt like the end of the world. Lights came on in Charles' house. I felt enormous excitement realising that he or someone he loved had turned them on.

I was surprised to see someone in the other car on the street, a Toyota SUV. He must have been reclining on the back seat or some-thing. I decided which of Charles' CDs to listen to. I decided on *The Cult Of Ray* because it was the one I liked least. I'd come to believe that the failing must be my own – that more attentive listening would make me as fond of it as I was of all his other stuff.

Two tracks from the end, somebody scared me out of the last

12 hours of my life by tapping on my passenger window – a guy in a Ralph Lauren windbreaker with binoculars around his neck, shiny pink skin, and an assistant bank manager's wire-rim glasses. He couldn't have looked less threatening on a bet, so I rolled the window down a few inches. "*Cult Of Ray*," he said self-delightedly. "Awesome, awesome album. How you doin'? Jim Pomeroy. From the RAV-4?"

He tried to figure out how to get his hand through the window for me to shake, but it wasn't open wide enough. I realised he was the Toyota SUV guy. I figured he might be some weird sort of cop or something, and didn't tell him my name, but only said, "How you doin'," back at him.

"Listen," he said, showing me his thermos, "I'm going to scoot over to 7-Eleven for some java. I was hoping you'd be able to keep a real good watch on the house for both of us while I'm gone. I won't be but ten minutes."

Java? Like coffee? I thought *Twin Peaks* was the only place anyone had ever actually called it that. Or maybe they'd called it joe. I had no idea what he was talking about, and it apparently showed.

"I'm staking out Chuck's place too," he explained, "just like every weekend night when he's not on the road. This'll be my fourth time. Haven't actually sighted him yet, but maybe tonight'll be the night, huh?" He guffawed. God, was he spooky.

"So we got a deal for the next few minutes, or what?" he asked grinningly.

"I'll be here," I said. I wasn't about to agree explicitly to a deal with this nutcase.

He drove away. Sure enough, he was back 10 minutes later. He'd not only filled up his own thermos bottle, but got me a big cup of . . . java of my own. Like I was really going to drink something this guy gave me.

It was as though he was reading my mind. "Oh, go on," he laughed. "I didn't put anything in it. The way I see it, we Chuckfans have to take care of each other." He waited for me, I thought, to invite him to hang out with me. When I didn't, he said, "Well, I'll be in the RAV. Just let me know if you need a potty break or anything."

I listened to *Black Letter Days* and *Surfer Rosa*. The light situation in

Charles' house didn't change. I'd never heard of anybody referring to him as Chuck. It began to bother me, and I'm too social a person just to sit somewhere listening to music if there's someone friendly nearby to talk to, so I paid Jim Pomeroy a visit.

He was ecstatic to see me. "Come on in," he said, turning down *Pistolero* and leaning over to unlock his passenger door. "Seriously. It's too nippy to stand out there. I'm not going to hassle you. Come on. It's nice and warm in here, and I've got some sandwiches if you want one. Egg salad. Homemade."

He was a bank manager. At work, he pretended to like the same stuff everybody else did – Dido and David Gray and so on – but he'd been a "heavy duty" Pixies and Chuck Thompson fan since first hearing *Doolittle* as a junior at the University of California at Davis, where he'd majored in business. He'd been to 61 Pixies and . . . Chuck shows over the years, and prided himself on never missing one within a 150-mile radius of Los Angeles. He didn't know what I meant about Charles' neighbourhood being desolate. It was very much like his own.

He wasn't sure what he'd do if Chuck ever came out to talk to him. He was pretty sure he'd get tongue-tied. The only other celebrity he'd ever met – well, not actually met, but pretty nearly bumped into – in a supermarket, around three years ago – was Tom Petty's drummer. At best, he figured he'd get Chuck to autograph a few CDs.

He asked what I'd do. I'd given it a lot of thought without coming to any firm conclusions. It had occurred to me that I might mention saving Joey Santiago's hands that night in Worcester, since Charles wouldn't have any way of knowing that the whole thing had been a hoax. I certainly wasn't going to do something as silly as ask for an autograph. I supposed I hoped Charles might invite me in, and I'd try to tell him in detail how much his music had always meant to me, and to poor Al too. Maybe we'd become friends. I'd make it very clear to his wife Jean that I had no romantic designs on him.

God, how very stupid of me. I realised that I should have brought something for Jean – chocolates or flowers or something – to demonstrate my honourable intentions. I excused myself, dashed to my rented car, drove over to the nearby 7-Eleven, the one where

Jim had apparently got his java, and bought three pairs of pantyhose, some cellotape and seriously overpriced gift wrap. It was either that or a bottle of wine, and I was afraid she might think the wine had really been for Charles, or poisoned. With pantyhose, there could be no confusion.

Back at the end of the cul-de-sac, all the same lights were on in Charles' house. I wrapped my gifts as best I could without a table to work on. I listened to *The Orange Album* and wondered what Jim was up to. My going over to see him seemed to give him a lot of pleasure. I got back in his SUV and told him about the present for Jean. He said he hoped I'd bought extra-large, as Jean, whom he'd glimpsed his second night, was just about as wide as she was high.

I asked how late he intended to stay. He said he usually tried to stay until at least two in the morning. "Which is what the java's for," he said, patting his thermos. He figured that Chuck kept a musician's hours. He thought there was a real chance of other musicians dropping by late at night for a jam session, and of Chuck popping over to 7-Eleven for a couple of six-packs. It was nearly eleven. I was jetlagged and tired.

We both jumped a couple of inches out of our seats when somebody tapped on Jim's window – a little roly-poly woman with curly red hair. "It's such a chilly night," she said with a slight Southern accent. "Why don't you all come on in?"

Jim looked at me in amazement. "Jean," he asked her, his voice shaking. "Jean Black?"

"Mary," she said, giggling with twinkly eyes. "Mary Collier. Mr. Thompson sold us his house it must be close to three months ago now. My understanding is that he's moved up to Portland, Oregon. I could give you the address I have all his mail forwarded to. And he gets an awful lot."

I think Jim and I both thought the same thing – that while it would hardly compare to actually meeting Charles, spending the night in the house he'd lived in would be a thrill all its own.

It was hard to imagine the house looking very much as it had when Charles and Jean lived in it. It was over-decorated to within an inch of its life, absolutely clogged with cute knick-knacks – pouting ceramic clowns and the like – and bric-a-brac, not that I was sure I could have told you the difference. There were several likenesses of Jesus, assuming Jesus had blue eyes and flowing auburn hair. Most of the furniture was covered in plastic. The place reeked of the potpourri scattered all around it. Music that made that at Al's mental ward seem like Nirvana in comparison played softly on the stereo.

Mary's husband – I assumed – Lorne was actually wearing a shirt and tie under his cardigan sweater, as though in a sitcom from the Fifties, the sort in which Pop was forever taking Junior, who looked very much like the very young Charles Thompson, aside to impart some essential moral lesson. He had more teeth than I'd ever seen in one place, and was grinning at us so as to give them all maximum exposure. "We're just tickled pink you dropped in," he said. I couldn't remember the last time I'd heard anyone described as tickled pink, though I seemed to recall the phrase peeking through the protective (of the viewer!) plastic in which *Hustler* magazine is sold in 7-Elevens.

I could have used a beer or even a shot, but our choices were between tea, coffee, decaf, and Diet Coke. I took the Diet Coke. We chatted. Lorne was 59, with two grown daughters from his previous marriage, which had ended with his wife's death, mention of which inspired Jim to murmur, "I'm so sorry," quite solemnly. Their friends liked to tease Lorne about being a cradle-robber because Mary was going to turn 34 in August. She was years younger than Charles, I thought, and could have been his grandmother. I was worried that she and Lorne thought me and Jim a couple, but even more worried that Jim seemed to think the same. He tried to reach under the table and hold my hand at one point. It was entirely too weird.

Jim had to be at his bank bright and early Monday morning, but I planned to drive my rental car up to Portland. I'd flown all the way to California to find Charles Thompson, and that's still what I intended to do.

"She's got some gumption, this one," Mary said admiringly.

"Don't I know it!" Jim agreed.

"Well, we've got church tomorrow," Lorne stood up to proclaim around 16 hours after I first began praying to be allowed to get to bed. Jim and I followed Mary down the hall to a little room that housed her doll collection. How had I known she'd have one? "This," she announced, "is the guest bedroom." There was one queen-sized bed in it. I was just about to say something when Jim, bless his heart, did it for me. "I guess I'll be out on the sofa then?" he wondered.

"We'll make it just as comfy for you as we can," Mary said. She'd known all along.

I was pleased to see the lock on the door. I could very easily picture Lorne trying to pay me a little visit when everyone else slumbered. I knew the type.

Sure enough, there was tapping on the door at a few minutes past three, according to the selfsame Casio wristwatch with which I'd used to time Frank Black & The Catholics songs for Al. "Lorne?" I said. "Jim? Whichever of you it is, I'm very sorry, but I'm not interested, OK?" There was no answer. "OK?" I repeated.

"Can't I come in for just two shakes, hon?" Mary whispered.

Just exactly what I needed – to fight off a little born-again lesbian at three in the morning in a guest bedroom I was sharing with 25,000 staring dolls in the most desolate suburb in America. "Actually, Mary," I said, "I was kind of sound asleep."

When she finally spoke again, after a silence so long I thought she might have waddled back to Lorne, what she said was, "Take me with you. Please."

I let her in. Her round pink face was streaked with tears. She put her arms around me and sobbed. "To Portland," she said. "I so want to go with you. Introduce me to interesting people, rock stars and what-have-you. I can share the driving. I have a learner's permit. I'll go crazy if I spend another week here with Lorne and his frigging – excuse my language! – potpourri and his doll collection and Jesus. I've tried – God knows I have! But I'll go bananas. Val, please."

If there's one thing I hate nearly as much as "little boys' room", it's bananas as a synonym for crazy. But I liked the idea of people affectionately shortening Valina to Val, and took her along just the same.

24

Catholic Tastes:
An Interview with Rich Gilbert

THE lavishly musical (he plays keyboards, pedal steel, and sax too) Catholics lead guitarist Rich Gilbert played with or for Throwing Muses, Tanya Donelly, Uncle Tupelo, and The Lemonheads before accepting Charles' invitation to become a Catholic, and, at the dawn of his professional career, Human Sexual Response. Within a year of joining The Catholics, he would become one of the mainstays of a wonderful country-oriented side project, The Blackstone Valley Sinners.

How did you start playing with Charles?
He called me out of the blue after Lyle [Workman] decided to stay in LA and not tour for a while. Charles and I go way back, I was in a great band called The Zulus that were popular in and around Boston when the Pixies first started playing around town. We did some shows together. I liked his approach and he liked mine, so a friendship and mutual admiration were formed. When he needed a new guitar player, he pretty much knew what he was going to get with me.

My understanding is that there was some resentment of the Pixies in the early Boston days because they made it so very quickly. True?
Probably by some, that's just how some people are going to be, you know? You work in shipping and receiving for five years and you see

the new employee who's been there for six weeks get promoted to department manager of jewellery and you feel a little jealous and envious and passed over. You can't blame a band for a rapid ascension to popularity, especially when they're a good band. But I never felt like "the scene" turned on them or anything like that.

What do you most admire about Charles' stuff?

Probably the same things everyone else who likes his music admires – interesting chord progressions and melodies, great lyrics. He just has that something extra that's hard to put your finger on that really talented artists have. If you talk about it too much or try to over-analyse it, you lose or destroy it. He is what he is.

How is working with Charles different from others who've employed you as a musician?

Well, I haven't really worked in many other situations where I've been hired to be in someone else's band – Steve Wynn. Tanya Donelly. Charles. Basically they all have given me tremendous freedom to bring what I have to the material. They've all asked me to play with them because they like my musical personality and style. The only difference with Charles is the material itself has more opportunities to take it to different places, so I guess with Charles I have the most freedom. But that's about it.

Lyle says he and Charles never exchanged an unpleasant word in more than five years together. Do you have a comparably harmonious relationship?

Charles and I do have a comparably harmonious relationship, although we traditionally have one pretty big fight during the recording of an album. Happens all the time within recording studios. There's nothing unusual about our head-butting – just two people with strong creative drives and ideas locking horns. The conflicts themselves aren't really that interesting or spectacular. I think we should go this way and he thinks we should go that way, and we fight about it. And then we settle it and go back to getting the music done, with no resentment or lingering bad vibes. There's never any residual tension afterwards however. We're always able to work out the conflict. It's good. It's exciting. It makes the music better.

We do get kind of loud, though, when it's blowing at full peak. I'm usually the loudest shouter. It's how I am. I've done it with every band I've been in and with every relationship I've had. When I blow, it's forceful and loud and intense, but usually done with in a couple of minutes.

Are you satisfied with your ability to help shape the FB&TC sound?

Sure. I'm given pretty much total freedom to do what I'm going to do with a song. Charles tends to work with musicians he admires and lets them bring their personality into the song. Duke Ellington did that also, you know. During live shows, for instance, sometimes I'll play a song on guitar but play it on keyboards or pedal steel on another night, whatever my mood is that evening. This also occurs during recordings. I may play guitar one day and if we record the same song later, I may try switching to piano or organ or something, just to see where it will lead. Of course the song gives you an idea of what it wants to be, but there's a lot of freedom to experiment with it and see what face or colour it ends up exhibiting.

To what tracks do you think you've made the greatest contribution? How?

That's hard to say. Probably the ones I don't play on – at least I don't get in the way. No, I can't say I feel I've contributed more or less to any tracks. I always try to provide the song with what it appears to need. Sometimes that's a lot of notes and music and action and fireworks all over the place and sometimes it's playing just four notes in the whole song, tops. It just depends on the song, which always tells you what to try if you pay attention.

How would you describe your and Dave Philips' relative strengths?

Well, we're stylistically very different players, which I think is our united strength. He covers ground that I don't and vice versa. You know, different people have different ways of saying things. He wears Dickies and I wear jeans. I favour boots and he's more of a low cut shoe kind of guy. He plays one way and I play another. He has his personality on the guitar and I've got mine. It's really that simple.

It's probably really just a generational difference. You hate to think it's true, but most people are somehow consciously or unconsciously influenced by the timeframe they were born into. I grew up in the Sixties and started playing guitar in the early Seventies so of course I was listening to people like Hendrix, Jimmy Page, Jeff Beck, Eric Clapton, Duane Allman, Carlos Santana, Steve Howe, John McLaughlin, etc. – basically the leaders of the field at the time – and I'm sure they all had an impact as to how I approach the instrument. Dave is younger than me, so he cut his teeth more in the early Eighties – you know, the glory days of indie rock and all the guitar antiheroes that were involved with that musical approach. So I would say that probably constitutes the main difference in our styles.

That isn't to say that I was only influenced by guitar players, which is most certainly not the case. I listened to all kinds of musicians and still do. But it does seem that, when you're starting out, the musicians you're tuned into at first have a major impact on your approach to the instrument.

I think we work very well together. We've played together enough now that there is an unspoken chemistry between us when we're playing. As a matter of fact though, I think that statement could be applied to The Catholics as a whole. We're all kind of ESPing with each other when we play. Songs change from night to night, depending on the mood of someone, or the mood of the band as a whole. Or the vibe of the room, or the crowd, or what you had for dinner. It could be one of a million things. We never use set lists when we play live, so all bets are off basically when we hit the stage. And I think it's better that way.

As far as my individual strengths are, I couldn't really say. I'm only aware of what my deficiencies are.

If you came up with a song that you thought would be a terrific addition to the FB&TC repertoire, would you feel free to present it to Charles?

Sure. In fact, Charles has encouraged me to do so, but it seems like most of the music I write isn't really FB&TC-style music – not that I'm sure what that even is. I have other outlets for what I do – Blackstone Valley Sinners. Coronet Premiers. Rich Gilbert & The Velvet Swingers. A couple of other bands I'm mulling putting together.

What's it like setting up and breaking down your own gear?

Well, let's face it, most musicians set up and break down their own gear and drive themselves to the gig, and take care of getting paid at the end of the night and work the merchandise booth and book the shows and change their own strings or drum heads and find a place to stay when they're on tour and change the tyre on the van when they have a blow-out in the middle of Nebraska. So what's the big deal? It's the super rare tiny minuscule percentage of musicians in the world that don't set up or break down their own gear.

So what's it like for me? I've been doing it most of my life. It's part of the job. I remember reading an interview with Paul Westerberg, back during The Replacements. He said something about how it's really discouraging when you're playing a show and you look over and see the guy who sets up and breaks down your amp and know he's getting paid more than you are. And for a lot of bands that's certainly the situation. Meanwhile, I can set up my own gear. Big deal.

Are you happy with the direct-to-stereo approach, or do you wish you could, for instance, layer guitars in harmony now and again?

We call it live-to-two-track. You've got to remember that, from the first Edison cylinder through the early Eighties, all music was recorded live, and some of it's pretty complex, like the Frank Sinatra/Nelson Riddle recordings in the Fifties, which is easily some of the best music ever recorded. You may not agree with me about that, but that's your problem. Listen again. Anyway, most of the time, live-to-two-track is fun. It makes you a better musician because you have to play it right, but with feeling and spontaneity. There's a lot of bands and musicians that just wouldn't be able to pull it off. But we can.

The downside is sometimes the version with your best guitar solo, or the best drum fills or the best piano playing doesn't get used because there's something else that doesn't jibe with that take. And since it's being mixed as it's being recorded, sometimes a nice detail can get somewhat obscured in the mix.

Again, I have other outlets for what I do, so I use multi-track recording in those situations. But you know what? It would also be nice to do a multi-track recording with The Catholics, just to see what comes out of it.

Charles has admitted he senses that the band is far less enthusiastic about some songs than others. Can you remember this being the case?

Actually, no, I can't think of a situation where it was obvious that everyone didn't like a song. Of course, someone is going to like one song more than another, and when you have four or more people working on a song, the odds are there's always going to be a song that isn't someone's favourite. I mean, fans and audience members like some songs more than others, so why should it be any different for the musicians? Even if you're having trouble with a song, you try to contribute something that will help make it stronger. And of course there arc times when everyone loves a particular song.

At the Shepherds Bush Empire in December 2003, you were the only member of the band who actually seemed to enjoy performing, and the only one who'd chosen his attire with any care.

The Shepherds Bush show was the final show of an arduous three-month European tour, so perhaps we were just burned out. But I pretty much always love playing live. I feel as though my brain is working at its peak capacity in a live situation – razor sharp. There are times when it's not going as smoothly, but I still feel extra alive and energised even during a rough show. I could easily be one of those musicians that plays 250–300 shows a year – you know, like James Brown or B.B. King.

As far as dressing for the show, I like wearing something particular and special – it puts my mind into a state of the show being a special moment to get ready and excited for. You know, sports players don't wear their street clothes when they play. Or actors. Or doctors. Lots of professions don't. And musicians didn't really until the whole alt-rock movement. Seems like the only people who criticise it or make a big deal out of it are indie rock veterans. Like it somehow devalues the music or makes it less "credible" or dishonest. Fuck that. That's bullshit.

Actually, some nights Charles will change clothes for the show and some nights he won't. It all depends on the mood of the day. If that's how he feels comfortable, then that's what he should do. I just possess a slightly more flamboyant approach perhaps. But there were a few tours where we all always wore finely tailored suits when we performed. Lately, Charles has also started favouring the well-crafted western shirt. Again, I can't speak for what he feels about it all, though I don't think the if-I-think-about-my-stage-attire-it-means-I'm-a-show-biz-phoney camp attitude applies.

Has the band ever considered trying to do something together without Charles, with one or more of you Catholics supplying the material?

No, not really. I think when I'm working on something else, I tend to want to work with different groups of musicians, just to take the music someplace else, and to bring out other facets of my playing. You need to put yourself into a place where you're not always comfortable to keep moving forward.

As a guitar player, what do you find most unusual or interesting about Joey Santiago's style and technique?

Everything! He's an incredibly singular player. Always comes up with something that is not the obvious approach, yet fits perfectly. Everyone has some form of technique, some like a hummingbird at 120 mph and some like a sea turtle, nice and easy and relaxed. I don't think Joey sets out to be "odd" or "unusual". He just comes up with ideas that someone else might overlook.

Too many musicians speak with their fingers first, not with their ears or mind or soul. That's why they don't play very well, although "technically" they may play great. But no one cares about what they have to say, or at least I don't. Joey always has something interesting to say. I think he and Charles have a really, really good natural musical chemistry.

Let's hear your best story about life on the road with FB&TC.

We were playing a small town in Oregon, a late afternoon show at a small art performance gallery-type space that probably only held about 150 people, if that, maybe only 100. There was no stage, and we just set up on the floor. And everyone in the audience was 18 and under with the general age being 15 and 17. And you know, kids at that age are pretty awkward and shy when they're not solely amongst their peers, especially when they're pretty excited inside. They were all quietly thrilled to be there to see Frank Black, but kind of nervous and shy about it.

In the middle of the set Charles stopped to introduce the band. When he got through introducing us, he said to the kid standing right in front of him, "And your name is . . .?" almost like a friendly, cool substitute teacher. The kid got all flustered, but also was blown away by the fact that he was being directly addressed by Charles – kids at that age worship artists that communicate something to them, but they never get to actually interact or speak with most of these artists. He finally came out with a shy "Bill". Charles then pointed to the girl next to Bill and said, "And you're . . .?" After the girl said Mary, he just had every kid there introduce themselves. And you could see these kids getting nervous but thrilled as the sequence was coming up to them. You could see they were so psyched that they were going to get to reply. These kids were just beaming about this.

The rest of the show was just charged with a great communal feeling. Those kids couldn't have been more thrilled. It was a really beautiful atmosphere,

25

It's Never Gonna Happen

BACK home just before Thanksgiving after spending the music festival season in good old reliable Europe, Charles unveiled some new songs at the Mint in LA, probably inspiring poor McCabe's to wonder if they'd said something to offend him. A grab-bag compilation of Frank Black B-sides appropriately entitled *Oddballs* became available online (at Emusic.com) and at the T-shirt stand at Frank Black & The Catholics shows. It contained only one unreleased track, the famous peppy 'Jumping Beans', which he'd played with They Might Be Frank. Elsewhere, 'At The End Of The World' mourned the passing of comedian John Candy. There was also a raucous version of Roxy Music's punk-anticipating 'Remake/Remodel', a cover of the Beau Brummels' 'Just A Little' notable for the background singing's audacity, and 'Man Of Steel', whose big ringing chords had earlier graced the *Songs In The Key Of X* [as in *X-Files*] compilation.

At the dawn of 2002, Charles played four solo shows in California clubs supporting the sublime Graham Parker. Once having completed his set each night, the tiny English ex-pat would graciously bring Charles back on stage to duet with him on The Ramones' 'Sheena Is A Punk Rocker'.

In the spring, Charles taped an appearance on VH-1's late-night variety show *Late World With Zach*, for broadcast on Grammy night. At the last minute, VH-1 decided to pre-empt Zach to provide coverage of the awards, even though anyone who knows anything at all regards the Grammys as a tired joke. Before they could reschedule

Charles' taped appearance, they cancelled the show entirely. Oh, the ignominy! Charles and Dave Philips and their wives played mutants in *Low Budget Time Machine*, which, at press time, had been seen exactly as often as the *Late World With Zach* appearance.

"We're doing a lot of rocking songs right now," Charles noted with pleasure, "like 'Solid Gold' and 'Freedom Rock' and 'Thalassocracy' and 'Wave Of Mutilation' – all these uptempo power rock numbers. Since we've been doing so much twang stuff, we haven't been doing so much of the loud rock, so we're enjoying that."

In July, the band had to cancel five shows in central and northern California when poor Scott Boutier was incapacitated. Salvation proved to have a familiar face. Mr. David Lovering, who'd been opening the show with his wacky magic routine, filled in for the Pomona and San Diego shows. In October, Charles opened what amounted to a late-Eighties alternative nostalgiafest for Gordon Gano of the Violent Femmes at the Troubadour, and then, hardly a month later, not only headlined at Winooski's Higher Ground, but also warbled a few songs and signed autographs at the town's hippest record store, Pure Pop, many of whose staff were almost certainly multiply pierced and tattooed.

Then, as though he hadn't had enough excitement, David Lovering came on stage at the end of the Bennies' support set at the Avalon in Boston to sing 'La La Love You' with his girlfriend. Of the very few punters present, several were seen to beam with pleasure at the sole live performance of the most nakedly sarcastic song in the Pixies canon.

Charles' returning as a matter of course now to the Winooskis of the world – to the stinking-of-stale-beer-but-four-pool-tables-for-your-convenience circuit – we pause to note, was very much a function of what a Fifties songwriter would invariably have described as foolish pride. Ken Goes was constantly hearing from promoters itching to put the re-formed Pixies on their stages, but Charles, with his famous knack for painting himself into corners, wouldn't have it, not even when there were substantial bucks involved, as when a big manufacturer of lawnmowers tried to entice the Pixies to play at their company picnic. "Maybe if we got to be the first band to perform a rock concert on the moon," he flippantly advised an interviewer who'd asked under what circumstances he'd consider a Pixies reunion. "I'd do it for the moon."

"It's OK if you're not in the big limelight," he was heard elsewhere to rationalise gamely, sticking implacably to his story. "Even if you're playing in some tiny club in the middle of nowhere, it's kind of like, 'Hey, guess what? I'm the one with a microphone and a guitar.' It's still a thrill."

"How can I [complain]?" he asked the *Washington Post*. "Because I don't have a bigger pile of money? That's a bad attitude when you make your living as a musician. Hey, you're in the club, you're on tour, you make records, you get to sing with David Bowie on his 50th birthday. What more do you want? An island?"

One Josh Frank, who'd earlier worked on the Nederlanders productions of *Love, Janis* (about Janis Joplin) and *Dream A Little Dream* (Mamas & Papas) succeeded in getting several major, major magazines to publish a press release about his intention to produce an off-Broadway play about Charles and the Pixies, entitled *Teenager Of The Year*. A fellow who'd ghost-written a manual entitled *How To Be A Porn Star* advised Ken Goes that he hoped to write a book about the Pixies, seemingly little realising what an unspeakable pill Ken could be, or how inaccessible the band.

Frank and The Catholics recorded their *Show Me Your Tears* direct to stereo on Charles' new mobile equipment. Because of its many reflections on the break-up of Charles' marriage, it reminded some of Bob Dylan's *Blood On The Tracks*. Surely there could be no mistaking that he'd taken to wearing his heart on his sleeve – or at least his influences. 'Everything Is New' is pure Springsteenian story-song – albeit not nearly as stirring as if the maestro himself had written and sung it. On 'The Snake', featuring a fab saxophone solo by Jack Kidney, he sounds as much like Lou Reed as like Mick Jagger on *Dog In The Sand*, and that's saying something. Most of the time he sounds substantially self-anaesthetised (that is, drunk), woozy with the pain of his shattered marriage. (If, as he suggests in the honky-tonk lament 'Horrible Day', it's really taken him to age 38 to feel for the first time in his life that he just don't care, though, he's led a charmed, charmed life, been fortune's shaven-headed boy after its fair-haired one. But we already knew that.)

The kick-off track, 'Nadine', sounds like something a 17-year-old who hasn't got the 12-bar format thoroughly mastered would write for his first garage band. The country-style road song 'My Favorite Kiss' isn't only pitched way too low for him, but is conspicuously badly written. "In seven days," he sings, "I'll be in Baltimore." The next line, "In two more weeks I'll be in . . ." should obviously end with a single syllable (Rome would do, or Nome). So which destination does Charles, still the avid shooter-of-self-in-foot choose? Dallas/Ft. Worth. Thus painting himself into a corner melodically.

He might be satirising New Age spiritualism on the unnotable 'Jaina Blues', and might not. Both 'This Old Heartache' and 'New House Of The Pope' are very successful imitations, conscious or otherwise, of Tom Waits' songwriting style. If only the band had rehearsed the latter a couple more times.

There's some fab pedal steel in 'Goodbye Lorraine', in which he drunkenly implores his departing lover to let him explain, but explains nothing, and some fab piano in 'When Will Happiness Find Me Again?' If he wasn't legless when these were recorded, he missed his calling not being a method actor. 'Massif Centrale' features a little scorcher of a guitar solo and a strong chorus, but he sings it horribly, if not as horribly as 'Manitoba', whose chorus he croaks, quite uglily. The liner notes list four supplementary singers, including the missus, but they keep a very low profile indeed.

All in all, probably the second best album of his post-Pixies career, which you may take in any way you please.

"I'm no Frank Black expert," wrote the ever-worshipful *Nude As The News*, "but I know what I like. I like the sound of a band properly aping classic rock song structures, the vibe of an album recorded live, in the moment, and the scream of a grown man gone wild. Conveniently, Monsieur Noir and his merry band of papists meet all of the above prerequisites and then some on *Show Me Your Tears* . . .

"As a point of reference, I request all readers pull out The Clash's *London Calling* and turn on 'Brand New Cadillac', the mad finish of which is not unlike the closing of 'Nadine'. No car or woman can drive a man to this point. Only the love of rock, my friends. And that's why this shit rules." Exactly the sort of bizarre, overheated approbation to which Charles must long since have grown accustomed!

Apparently having noted that his music was rarely getting reviewed anywhere but on the Internet anymore, Charles claimed, "I'm happy that critics write about me, even if they're giving me bad reviews. As long as they're writing about me I guess it's a good sign." An unlikely proclamation from one who, not two years later, wouldn't trouble himself to send a simple email of acknowledgement to one he'd heard had been commissioned to write a whole book about his life and work – one who appealed repeatedly to the originally very encouraging, but later surly Goes, pointing out that everyone concerned, from the little people shivering in the ticket queues to Charles himself, was likely to be happier with a book that related his story accurately and completely instead of relying on wild vituperation and hyperbole in an often desperate attempt to keep the reader diverted.

In 2003, Charles not only showed no sign of slowing down, but actually sped up, to the tune of 143 shows, in-store appearances, and radio interviews.

It may seem wonderfully serendipitous that he would begin a year during which he would admit to having benefited from psychotherapy with three nights at the Freud Playhouse at the University of California, Los Angeles. But the Playhouse was named in honour of a UCLA theatre arts professor, and not Clement.

As though he hadn't enough on his plate, Charles (or someone who looked and sounded exactly like him, and had gone to the trouble of learning his repertoire), played a couple of impromptu solo shows, one of them at Sam Bond's Garage in Eugene, where it had all begun, all those years before. And this after having performed at Louie in Saskatoon, Saskatchewan, mere weeks earlier! He did his celebrated hail-fellow-well-met thing on some key UK and Irish radio shows – one interviewer memorably described his manner as that of "an LA suburbanite who enjoys a good barbecue and knows everything there is to know about cars" – and, for once, didn't confine himself to the usual salubrious countries, but ventured into Warsaw.

When he went home, it was to Portland, in which he was unashamed to be living what he called The Loft Lifestyle with a new lover. To nearly everyone's astonishment, he began hedging on the question of whether the Pixies might ever regroup.

Over the years, his denial of the possibility of a Pixies reunion had ranged from the gentle ("It seems cooler not to get the Pixies back together. It seems cooler to keep it in the past.") to the rather pointed ("It just doesn't interest me. I've graduated from that particular class. It's like being asked if you want to go back to the 10th grade, and you're like, 'No, I'm in high school now.') to the vitriolic ("It's never gonna happen. I can say that the day the Pixies do a reunion tour is the day after I'm dead.").

He seemed very much alive, though, when he confided during an interview with London radio station XFM that the group has been getting together every once in a while to play informally, as they were rumoured to have done on New Year's Eve, 2002, in Sedona, Arizona, of all places.

He seemed no less alive on February 9, 2004, when the Western world woke to the news that the group would the play the first of 11 North American headlining dates in Winnipeg on Wednesday, April 14. The two bookings in Saskatchewan (at Prairieland!) suggested that there'd been a method in Charles' earlier madness! The tour was to conclude with a big deluxe May Day performance at the Coachella Festival in Indio, California.

Many wondered if Charles, in a brilliant satirical move, would announce his intention neither to play any of his post-Pixies material nor even to speak the name Catholics during the tour. There was talk that the group would be performing new material, in addition to the old favourites. It got out that none other than Charles' old champion at American Recordings, Marc Geiger, now senior vice president of William Morris, was doing their booking.

So did the reunited indie idols throw their arms around one another and weep unashamedly when they convened? Not a chance. They compared their various orders from Starbucks, as indicated by the boxes ticked on the paper ring around the styrofoam cups.

Indeed, it was Charles' impression that none of them had changed in the slightest. When they strapped on their instruments, he discovered that he had, until the musical equivalent of muscle memory kicked in, to get Joey or Kim to remind him how to play songs he himself had composed all those years ago.

They announced plans to visit good old reliable Europe. Tickets for their two performances at the Brixton Academy in London sold out in only slightly longer than it's taken you to read this sentence. Two more nights were added, and they sold out instantly too. Then Geiger announced that he was booking an autumn–December tour of Major American Markets, some with venues seating as many as 10,000. The smart money was on Charles not having to set up his own amplifier anymore for a while – and on the poor Catholics not being ecstatic about twiddling their thumbs for the next eight months.

If Winooski was heartbroken not to be included on the tour itinerary, it kept it well hidden.

Postscript

ONCE having coaxed Charles back into the fold, the Pixies performed through the last three-quarters of 2004 as though trying to make up for lost time. They played three weeks' worth of shows in Canadian prairie cities and in the Northwest, and then at the Coachella Festival in the southern California desert. Thirty-dollar tickets for the first shows were offered (and, apparently, bought) on eBay for $400.

When advised that the Pixies would be lower-billed than Radiohead at the Coachella Festival, Thom Yorke, the sort of fan for whom every band prays, howled as though shocked by electricity: "No! That's just not right! The Pixies opening for us is like The Beatles opening for us. I won't allow it. There's no way we can follow the Pixies!" A week later, the Pixies were in Brazil, at the Curitiba Pop Festival, and a couple of weeks later in Reykjavik, Iceland. They played four sold-out, rapturously received shows at London's Brixton Academy, and then headed for the European festival circuit, pausing en route to do their first gig ever at a Slovenian monastery, Ljubljana's Krizanke. 'Twas a proofreader's worst nightmare made flesh! They co-headlined the V Festival in Chelmsford with The Strokes and signed on to play North American venues through the first week in December.

What a spectacle! At one of the Brixton gigs, a fan (albeit not Jude Law, who was there) was overheard to exclaim, "Blimey, he looks like a Chelsea supporter!" when Charles materialised on stage. Kim, for her own part, looked like the sort of thickish matron who'd be more at home rasping pre-ontologically with fellow moms in the concession wagon at their sons' Babe Ruth League baseball game, losing the ash of her cigarette into the grilled onions as she reached for a fresh brewski.

But their audiences seemed to adore them, not least, many observed, because they stuck exclusively to their early stuff – three-quarters of each of the first two albums, and several songs from *The Purple Tape/Come On Pilgrim*. Though comprising large numbers of fans too young to have been around in the early days, their audiences were routinely observed bellowing along no less rapturously to 'Broken Face' than to 'Here Comes Your Man'. Charles occasionally enjoyed himself so much as to wax playful, here making little antlers of his fingers in 'Caribou', there beaming at La Deal. Joey, whose hairline seemed to be making for the back of his head, and whose waistline seemed to idolise Charles', still barely moved on stage. Lovering, who'd let his curly hair grow long, got to sing 'La La Love You' each night.

Absolutely nobody was heard hollering requests for Frank Black favourites, but you had to hand it to Charles, not turning to drink, opium, or loose women in the face of the world essentially having told him that it adored the music he'd made 16 years and more in the past, but hadn't much interest in that which he'd made since.

The first new Pixies studio recording since 1991, Kim's *Bam Thwok*, came to be downloadable from iTunes. It turned out that the band had recorded it at a little studio in LA shortly after confirming that they'd be performing together again. Through the miracle of modern digital recording, the track incorporated an organ solo Joey's father-in-law had recorded many years before, while doing mission-ary work in the Philippines. It came out also that Charles had been working on a double solo album at the time of the Pixies' reconcilia-tion, one disc apparently to consist of our hero reinventing Pixies classics with the help of the way arty Two Pale Boys, the other of Charles' pre-Pixies solo demos. A must for collectors!

But the world would just have to wait. For the time being, Charles seemed to be getting too much pleasure out of getting seriously rich, and having somebody else set up his amplifier.

Acknowledgements

Thanks to the following for their kind help in the preparation of this wee tome: Gavin Boucher, Steve Crawford, Anthony Durazzo, Jop Euwijk, Rich Gilbert, Dan Kramer, Carlos Lopez, Kylie Minogue, Gil Norton, Mark Paytress, Martin van Rappard, Chris Sharp, and Lyle Workman.

Special thanks to Chris Charlesworth, without whom you wouldn't be reading this.

I urge Pixies and Frank Black fans to visit these excellent websites, which I plundered rapaciously over the course of my research:

Jean-Michel Biel's and Christophe Gourraud's superb Alec Eiffel (aleceiffel.free.fr/)

Frank Black Net (www.frankblack.net)

123456789